2nd Edition

How to Probate an Estate

- A Step-By-Step Guide for Executors

by enodare publishing

Bibliographic Data:

- International Standard Book Number (ISBN): 978-1-906144-61-6
- Printed in the United States of America
- Second Edition: January 2014

Published By: Enodare Limited
                            Athlone
                            Co. Westmeath
                            Ireland

Printed & Distributed By: International Publishers Marketing
                                 22841 Quicksilver Drive
                                 Dulles, VA 20166
                                 United States of America

For more information, e-mail books@enodare.com.

Warning & Disclaimer

Although precautions have been taken in the preparation of this book, neither the publisher nor the author assumes any responsibility for errors or omissions. No warranty of fitness is implied. The information is provided on an "as is" basis. The author and the publisher shall have neither liability nor responsibility to any person or entity with respect to any loss or damages (whether arising by negligence or otherwise) arising from the use of or reliance on the information contained in this book or from the use of any forms accompanying it.

IMPORTANT NOTE

This book is meant as a general guide to probating an estate. While effort has been made to make this book as accurate as possible, laws and their interpretation are constantly changing. As such, you are advised to update this information with your own research and/or counsel and to consult with your personal legal, financial and medical advisors before acting on any information contained in this book.

The purpose of this book is to educate and entertain. It is not meant to provide legal, financial, taxation or medical advice or to create any attorney-client or advisory relationship. The authors and publisher shall have neither liability (whether in negligence or otherwise) nor responsibility to any person or entity with respect to any loss or damage caused or alleged to be caused directly or indirectly by the information or documents contained in this book or the use of that information or those documents.

ABOUT ENODARE

Enodare, the international self-help publisher, was founded in 2000 by a group which included lawyers, entrepreneurs, business professionals, authors and academics. Our aim was simple - to provide access to quality business and legal products and information at affordable prices.

Enodare's Will Writer software was first published in that year and, following its adaptation to cater for the legal systems of over 30 countries worldwide, quickly drew in excess of 40,000 visitors per month to our website. From this humble start, Enodare has quickly grown to become a leading international self-help publisher with legal and business titles in the United States, Canada, the United Kingdom, Australia and Ireland.

Our publications provide customers with the confidence and knowledge to help them deal with everyday issues such as setting up a company, running a business, preparing a tenancy agreement, making a last will and testament and much more.

By providing customers with much needed information and forms, we enable them to protect both themselves and their families through the use of easy-to-read legal documents and forward planning techniques.

The Future….

We are always seeking to expand and improve the products and services we offer. However, in order to do this, we need to hear from interested authors and to receive feedback from our customers.

If something isn't clear to you in our publications, please let us know and we'll try to make it clearer in the next edition. If you can't find the answer you want and have a suggestion for an addition to our range, we'll happily look at that too.

USING SELF-HELP BOOKS

Before using a self-help book, you need to carefully consider the advantages and disadvantages of doing so – particularly where the subject matter is of a legal or tax related nature.

In writing our self-help books, we try to provide readers with an overview of the laws in a specific area. While this overview is often general in nature, it provides a good starting point for those wishing to carry out a more detailed review of a topic.

However, unlike an attorney advising a client, we cannot cover every conceivable eventuality that might affect our readers. Within the intended scope of this book, we can only cover the principal areas in a given topic and even where we cover these areas, we can still only do so to a moderate extent. To do otherwise would result in the writing of a text book which would be capable of use by legal professionals. This is not what we do.

We try to present useful information and documents that can be used by an average reader with little or no legal knowledge. While our sample documents can be used in the vast majority of cases, everybody's personal circumstances are different. As such, they may not be suitable for everyone. You may have personal circumstances which might impact the effectiveness of these documents or even your desire to use them. The reality is that without engaging an attorney to review your personal circumstances, this risk will always exist. It's for this very reason that you need to consider whether the cost of using a do-it-yourself legal document outweighs the risk that there may be something special about your particular circumstances which might not be taken into account by the sample documents attached to or referred to in this book (or indeed any other sample documents).

It goes without saying (we hope) that if you are in any doubt as to whether the documents in this book are suitable for use in your particular circumstances, you should contact a suitably qualified attorney for advice before using them. Remember the decision to use these documents is yours! We are not advising you in any respect.

In using this book, you should also take into account the fact that this book has been written with the purpose of providing a general overview of the laws in the United States. As such, it does not attempt to cover all of the various procedural nuances and specific requirements that may apply from state to state – although we do point some of these out along the way. Rather, in our book, we try to provide forms which give a fair example of the type of forms which are commonly used in most states. Nevertheless, it remains possible that your state may have specific requirements which have not been taken into account in our forms.

Another thing that you should remember is that the law changes – thousands of new laws are brought into force every day and, by the same token, thousands are repealed or amended every day! As such, it is possible that while you are reading this book, the law might well have been changed. Let's hope it hasn't but the chance does exist! Needless to say, we take regular steps (including e-mail alerts) to update our customers about any changes to the law. We also ensure that our books are reviewed and revised regularly to take account of these changes.

Anyway, assuming that all of the above is acceptable to you, let's move on to exploring the topic at hand..............probating an estate!

TABLE OF CONTENTS

Chapter 3: Executor's Duties: What to Do Immediately After Death... 55

Chapter 4: Making Sense of the Will and What To Do If There isn't One 69

AN INTRODUCTION TO PROBATE

Probating an estate requires a lot more from an executor than simply writing checks and handing over the assets of a deceased person to his or her named beneficiaries. It can be a demanding and time consuming task involving complicated taxes, fee payments, disputes amongst beneficiaries and tricky asset transfers. It's therefore important that you are properly prepared for the task before embarking on it. This preparation can take the form of reading one or more books, such as this one, as well as engaging the services of an experienced estate planning or probate attorney to assist you in navigating this sometimes difficult process.

 Did You Know?

In many states, executors are referred to as "personal representatives". Someone who manages an estate without a will is an "administrator". In this book, we will use the terms interchangeably but will mostly use the word "executor" for convenience. A person named in a will to receive assets may be known as a "beneficiary" or "devisee" while a person entitled to inherit where there is no will is often called an "heir." We will use the term "beneficiary" to refer to anyone entitled to inherit a part of the probate estate.

Probate itself can be described as a court supervised process by which a deceased person's net property is transferred to the beneficiaries named in his will. If the deceased person died without a valid will, this process will be known as an 'administration' rather than a probate.

Every state has its own set of probate laws (often referred to as the probate code) which set out the specific rules and procedures for probate and administration in that state. These laws typically set out the requirements for a will to be deemed valid and tell us things such as who is in charge of the deceased's estate after he dies, who is entitled to receive assets from that estate if the deceased hasn't made a valid will, which creditors need to be paid upon the deceased's death and in what order of priority, how and when to distribute assets, and so on.

While an attorney is not required to assist you with the probate process, the right probate attorney could help you maintain control over the costs of winding up the deceased's estate - thereby ensuring that those costs are kept to a minimum. A good attorney could also save you countless hours of work and relieve you of much of the stress that can sometimes be associated with the probate process.

However, an executor's role is often not a complex one. Therefore, with proper preparation, most people should be able to conduct much if not all of the process without the assistance of an attorney.

The first step in the probate process will usually involve the person named as an executor in a will actually locating a copy of the deceased's will and proving to the probate court that it is in fact the last will of the deceased and, more importantly, that it is valid. This process normally requires the presentation of the will to the court. Some states may also require the production of simple affidavits from the people who witnessed the deceased signing his will. Once the court confirms the validity of the will, the nominee executor can be formally appointed by the court as the executor or personal representative of the deceased's estate. When this happens, the executor will become responsible for the location, collection and distribution of the deceased's assets.

Once the executor has collected and valued the assets of the deceased's estate and determined the level of debt owed by the estate, he will be able to determine whether the net value of the deceased's estate is small enough to undergo the simplified probate procedures which exist in many states (we cover this in more detail in later chapters) and whether any income, estate or death taxes are owed by the estate. He will also be charged with ensuring that any debts owed by the deceased at the time of his death are paid from the estate assets.

When all of the estate's assets have been collected and its debts and taxes paid, the executor will distribute the assets of the estate to the beneficiaries named in the deceased's will. Once done, he will file the relevant forms and accounts with the probate court summarizing the actions he has taken as executor - and that's it, job done!

The entire process can be long and often takes 12 months or more to complete. Of course, if complications arise this process may end up dragging on for years! For this reason, executors should always consider contacting an attorney if something unexpected occurs during the probate process. This may end up saving the estate unnecessary costs and delays; not to mention saving the executor hours of work.

This Book and You!

This book is designed to guide would-be executors step-by-step through the probate process and to give you the knowledge and confidence to act as an executor if you are asked to fulfill the role — or even to offer to take on the role if you haven't. On the other hand, if you reach the end of this book and still feel disinclined to take on the job of executor — you will have a fund of knowledge which will enable you to discuss the subject intelligently with other people and guide others through the process.

CHAPTER 1:
OVERVIEW OF PROBATE AND THE EXECUTOR'S ROLE

Chapter Overview

In this chapter, we take a brief look at the probate process and the role of executors and personal representatives generally. Having read this chapter, you will have a good understanding of the probate process and the executor's role.

Chapter

1

CHAPTER 1

OVERVIEW OF PROBATE AND THE EXECUTOR'S ROLE

What is Probate and How is it Commenced?

Historically, the word 'probate' was a term used to describe the process by which the validity of a deceased person's last will and testament was determined. In more recent times, however, it has come to include the entire administrative process surrounding the collection of the deceased's assets, the payment of his debts and the passing of his property to his beneficiaries.

The person responsible for carrying out this administrative process is called an 'executor' or a 'legal representative'.

Important Note

A 'testator' is the name given to a person who makes a last will and testament. From time to time, you will also see the female version of the word, 'testatrix', used. However, in most cases, the word 'testator' is used.

One of the first tasks facing you as an executor will be to locate the deceased's last will and testament. Not only will it set out how the deceased wanted to have his estate distributed, it will also confirm that you have in fact been nominated as the executor of the deceased's estate. Once you have found the will, your next task will be to determine whether it has been validly executed. To this end, you will need to ensure, for example, that it has been signed by the deceased testator and witnessed by the correct number of witnesses. The laws in most states require that at least two people witness the testator signing his will and that they acknowledge that by subscribing their names as witnesses on the will itself. In some states, such as Vermont, the law requires that there be at least three witnesses. Other states, such as Colorado, can be more forgiving and permit probate of a will or "will substitute" even if there are not enough witnesses or other formalities have not been met.

Having determined that the will has in fact been validly signed and witnessed, the next step will be for you to determine whether that will is in fact the last will and testament of the deceased. The reason for this is that only the last will of the deceased has any legal effect - as the making of a new will generally tends to revoke old wills in their entirety. It's for this reason that it's important that a testator physically destroys any pre-existing wills and codicils when he makes a new will. By doing this, he will lessen the possibility of confusion and argument arising as to which will is in fact the testator's last will.

Assuming that you have located the deceased's last will and that it is properly executed and witnessed, you will then need to determine whether probate is required. If so, you will need to make the relevant application to commence probate, and to have 'letters of authority' issued to you by the probate court.

Letters of Authority

In order to officially appoint someone to wind-up a deceased person's estate, the probate court will issue a formal letter of appointment. In practice, there are three forms of letters of appointment that are most commonly issued. These include the following:

1.   Letters of authority

      Letters of authority (sometimes called 'letters testamentary') is the name given to the document issued by the probate court confirming the appointment of an executor named in the deceased's will. The letters authorize the named executor to administer the estate of the deceased in accordance with the terms of the deceased's will.

2. Letters of administration (with will annexed)
    These letters are issued when the deceased has made a will and (i)
    has either failed to nominate an executor in that will or (ii) the person
    nominated as executor in the will is unable or unwilling to act as
    executor. In this case, the rules of intestacy will apply to determine who
    is entitled to be appointed as the executor of the deceased's estate.

3. Letters of administration
    Letters of administration are issued when the deceased has either
    not made a will or has made a will that turns out to be invalid. In that
    case, the rules of intestacy will again determine who is entitled to be
    appointed as administrator of the deceased's estate.

 Did You Know?

The 'rules of intestacy' are a set of legal rules that each state has to
determine (i) who will be entitled to receive the property of a deceased
person if that person dies without having made a last will and (ii) who will
be entitled to act as the administrator (which is like an executor) of the
deceased's estate.

Each of the letters of authority allows the person named as executor therein to
represent the deceased's estate for the purpose of winding it up. In the majority
of cases, the issuing of letters of authority is merely an administrative process.
However, before a prospective executor applies to have letters of authority
issued to him, he should satisfy himself as to whether they are in fact needed
and have a clear understanding of the reasons why.

Why are Letters of Authority Necessary?

When a person dies, he may (for example) have money sitting in bank or
brokerage accounts at the time of his death. These monies will need to be
transferred to the deceased's estate so that they can be used to discharge
debts of the estate or, as the case may be, distributed by the executor to the

beneficiaries of the estate. However, before a financial institution can transfer these monies, it will need to satisfy itself that the person claiming the monies on behalf of the deceased's estate is lawfully entitled to do so.

The letters of authority issued by the probate court provide evidence of the executor's legal entitlement to claim and receive monies on behalf of the deceased's estate. The production of these letters to financial institutions allows them to lawfully pay over the monies held in a deceased customer's account to the person named as executor/administrator in the letters. Any payment made by the financial institution to this named person will be a good discharge of the institution's duties and obligations to pay the monies to the deceased's estate. After that, the distribution of these monies to the correct people is the responsibility of the executor of the deceased's estate and not the financial institution which held the monies.

Insurance companies holding proceeds of insurance on behalf of a deceased policy holder will also need to evidence the entitlement of the executor to receive those proceeds on behalf of the deceased's estate. The insurance companies will do this in the same manner as outlined for financial institutions above.

The term "personal representative" is commonly used instead of the term "executor" in the following states:		
Alaska	Maine	North Dakota
Arizona	Michigan	South Carolina
Colorado	Minnesota	South Dakota
Florida	Montana	Utah
Hawaii	Nebraska	Wisconsin
Idaho	New Mexico	

Are Letters of Authority Always Needed?

Letters of authority may not be needed where:

    (i)   the net value of the deceased's estate is small enough for it to be classified as a "small estate" within the meaning of local probate laws; or

    (ii)   the assets held by the deceased can be transferred to beneficiaries of the deceased without going through the probate process.

We discuss each of these aspects in more detail in later chapters.

In addition, letters of authority may also not be needed where organizations are willing to release monies they hold in the deceased's name without production of the letters. However, such organizations will invariably attach other conditions to the release of the funds such as the requirement to produce a certified copy of the deceased customer's death certificate. The organization may even require that the proceeds of the account be transferred into a specific account such as one in the name of the deceased customer's spouse. It follows that, where the amount of funds held by the organization on behalf of the deceased is relatively small, it may be worth investigating whether the organization in question would be willing to release the funds in the absence of producing the letters of authority.

By contrast, an executor will need to obtain and produce letters of authority in order to formally transfer or sell assets registered in the deceased's name if those assets have formal legal titles - such as in the case of real estate or stocks, for example.

 Important Note

If you are in any doubt as to the type of letters that need to be issued in connection with the winding up of a deceased person's estate or whether letters of authority are in fact required at all, speak to your lawyer. As an executor, you will be entitled to engage an attorney to assist you in winding up the deceased's estate. The costs of that attorney will be borne by the estate and not by you personally.

Persons Entitled to Apply for Letters of Authority

There are some basic rules which determine the priority in which people are entitled to apply to the probate court for the issue of letters of authority to them. While these rules of priority vary slightly from state to state, people are usually entitled to apply for letters in the following order: -

- firstly, the person(s) named as executor(s) under the deceased's will;

- secondly, the person(s) named as alternate executor(s) under the deceased's will;

- thirdly, the surviving spouse of the deceased or a proposed executor nominated in writing by the spouse;

- fourthly, beneficiaries named in the deceased's will or their nominee; with the rule of thumb being that the beneficiary entitled to receive the largest share of the deceased's estate will have priority;

- fifthly, the deceased's next-of-kin or heirs-at-law (who are not beneficiaries) or their nominee; and

- sixthly, creditors of the deceased; with the rule of thumb being that the creditor with the largest share of the debts owing by the deceased will have priority.

The list of priority above is a general guide. As such, to determine the precise entitlements of people to apply for letters of authority, you will need to check the terms of the deceased's will carefully to see whether an executor was nominated, who the beneficiaries are, the size of their shares, etc, and the probate laws of the state in which the deceased was resident at the time of his death.

Restrictions on Who Can Be an Executor

While there are very few restrictions on who can serve as an executor, there are some. For example, a person will not be entitled to act as an executor if they are under the age of majority in the state in which the probate is being carried on. Similarly, persons who have been convicted of a felony or who are not U.S. citizens may not be permitted to take on the role of an executor.

Out-of-State Executors

Restrictions on who can act as an executor also apply where a person living outside the deceased's state of residence is named as an executor of the deceased's estate. In such cases, state laws impose a number of different requirements on such persons and these requirements must be met before they can lawfully act as executors. For example, in order for an out-of-state resident to be an executor in many states, they must first:

(i) be a relative of the deceased;

(ii) be a primary beneficiary under the deceased's will; or

(iii) post an insurance bond to ensure that the beneficiaries under the will are protected against potential wrongdoings by them.

While many states allow testators to include a clause in their will which effectively waives the requirement to have their proposed executor put a bond in place, a number of states do not permit this type of waiver and require that bonds be put in place. The costs of these bonds can turn out to be quite expensive particularly where the estate is large.

As the restrictions in relation to the appointment of out-of-state executors vary from state to state, it is important that you check the laws of the state in which the probate is being carried out to see if any restrictions apply in your case.

Getting Appointed & What to Do Next

In order to formalize his appointment, the potential executor will need to file an application for probate. This application will include a copy of the deceased's last will and testament. Once filed, the probate court will formally rule on the validity of the will. More often than not, this is just a 'rubber-stamp affair'. If there are any challengers to the validity of the will they will be required to present their objections to the court within a specific time frame. This time frame will vary from state to state. If no successful challenges are made within the required time frame, the court will move to make its final ruling on the validity of the deceased's will.

If the court deems the will valid and accepts the applicant's appointment as executor, it will issue letters of authority to the executor. Once these letters have been issued, the executor may begin the process of paying estate taxes, settling debts with creditors and other claims against the deceased's estate, and then distributing the remaining assets of the estate to the beneficiaries named in the deceased's will.

Important Note

Generally, the laws governing the probate of the deceased's estate will be the laws of the state in which the deceased was ordinarily resident at the time of his death.

If, for some reason, the will is found to be invalid it will be necessary to proceed on the basis that the deceased died intestate. In that case, the court will appoint an administrator to administer the estate. This may or may not be the person named in the deceased's will (assuming an executor was in fact named in the will) depending on the laws governing the probate of the deceased's estate.

Once all of the debts and taxes have been paid and the deceased's assets distributed, the final step in the probate process will be the filing of the requisite forms, papers and accounts in the probate court. These papers will include an account of everything done by the executor in probating the estate as well as an accounting of all of the assets that formed part of the estate; details of the monies paid by the estate and why; copies of all notices and tax returns issued, received or filed in connection with the estate, and so on. The executor will also be expected to provide proof of the distribution of the deceased's assets to the correct beneficiaries. This proof usually takes the form of signed acknowledgements of receipt from the beneficiaries. The papers may also include copies of deeds transferring the deceased's real property to the relevant beneficiaries as well as instruments of distribution in respect of the deceased's personal property.

As soon as the court acknowledges that the executor has successfully completed all of the required steps in the administration of the deceased's estate, he will be formally released by the court from any further duties and obligations as executor of the deceased's estate.

How Long Does Probate Take?

The time required to probate an estate will depend very much on the level of assets and liabilities of the estate and whether or not the deceased's affairs were in order at the time of his death. If the deceased's estate is complicated, it could take a considerable period of time to determine precisely what assets were held and what debts and taxes were owed by the deceased at the time of his death. Once that determination is made, it will take time to collect in those assets and to pay those debts and taxes.

Even where the estate is not complex, delays may still arise. For example, time may be spent locating assets or beneficiaries, dealing with legal challenges to the validity of the deceased's will itself, appointing and removing executors, seeking court guidance and so on. All of these will draw out the length of the probate process.

Taking all of factors into account, the average probate can take anywhere from six months to a year to complete. For example, the average time taken to probate an estate in California is eight months. However, if there are major complications, probate can continue for years and even decades.

In most cases, however, probate will be completed within a period of one year from the filing of the initial application for probate. This period is typically referred to as the 'executor's year'. If probate has not been completed within that period, the executor may be required to file a status report with the probate court. This report will set out details of what still needs to be done to complete the probate and include an estimate of how much time it's likely to take to carry out those outstanding tasks.

If an executor fails to file a status report, the beneficiaries named in the deceased's will can petition the court to make an order (i) requiring the executor to file the report and (ii) take such other actions as it deems necessary to bring about the proper closure of probate including the removal of the executor and the appointment of someone else in his place.

How Much Will Probate Cost?

The cost of probate differs from place to place and is generally determined by either state law or custom and practice in a particular area. However, on average, the total cost of probate usually amounts to between one and seven per cent of the gross value of the deceased's estate. As some of these probate costs are set by state law there is very little that can be done to mitigate or reduce them - other than to avoid the probate process itself.

Certain states, such as California for example, have legislation which sets out the maximum fees that a lawyer can charge for probating an estate. These maximum fees are based on the gross value of the estate. By gross value, we mean the total value of the estate before any debts or liabilities are subtracted from the estate. As such, these fees can be quite high. Consider for example a case where the principal asset of the estate was a property worth $1 million with a mortgage of $900,000 secured against that property. Notwithstanding that the net realizable value of the asset on a sale is only $100,000, the attorney will be able to charge fees based on a percentage of $1 million. Based on the table on page 30, this will result in legal fees of $23,000 for something with a net value of $100,000!

Needless to say, if someone contests the will or if there is any litigation in relation to the estate assets, there is no way to determine by how much those costs could increase. The table on page 30, which is based on the California probate code, will give you a good idea of likely statutory probate costs. These fees represent the maximum fees that a lawyer can charge assuming that there are no unusual taxes or legal issues associated with the probate.

Probate Legal Fees California

Estate Value	Statutory Fee
$100,000	$4,000
$200,000	$7,000
$300,000	$9,000
$400,000	$11,000
$500,000	$13,000
$600,000	$15,000
$700,000	$17,000
$800,000	$19,000
$900,000	$21,000
$1,000,000	$23,000
$2,000,000	$33,000

By contrast, in New York, probate fees are payable at the rate of 5% on the first $100,000 of the estate, 4% on the next $200,000, 3% on the next $700,000, 2.5% on the next $4 million and 2% on the rest.

You should check the amount of probate fees chargeable in your state.

Do You Need a Lawyer?

If the deceased's estate is not complex and you are prepared to (i) do some research and (ii) put in the time and effort necessary to probate the deceased's estate, then you should be able to complete the probate without instructing a lawyer. In fact, people regularly probate estates without engaging lawyers. In other cases, people engage lawyers merely to watch over their shoulder as they go through the process.

However, because mistakes have the potential of causing delays and increasing costs, most executors engage lawyers to assist them with the probate process. An experienced lawyer will immediately know what needs to be done to probate an estate, will have come across pretty much every conceivable problem that could arise during the probate process, will be able to ensure that all the procedural requirements are complied with and that there are no unnecessary delays in the process.

If, having read this book and done some research, you feel confident enough to take on the process alone, you are perfectly free to do so. However, if you are in any doubt as to what needs to be done, we recommend that you consult a lawyer. A wrong decision or a misunderstanding on your part could cause major delays in the process, as well as exposing you to actions for negligence if the wrongdoing on your part causes a loss to the estate. As such, while it's not necessary to engage a lawyer, it can often be very beneficial in terms of ensuring a smooth and quick winding up of the estate and protecting you from allegations and claims of wrongdoings.

The final decision to become an executor is of course yours to make!

CHAPTER 2:
DUTIES AND RESPONSIBILITIES OF EXECUTORS

Chapter Overview

In this chapter, we will give you an idea of some of the main duties, responsibilities and liabilities facing executors. These should all be taken into consideration before deciding whether to accept the role.

Chapter 2

CHAPTER 2

DUTIES AND RESPONSIBILITIES OF EXECUTORS

 Important Note

You should carefully consider all relevant factors before deciding to take on the role of executor. Don't simply accept the role out of a sense of obligation. You must be both comfortable with and willing to perform the tasks associated with the role.

Responsibilities of an Executor

An executor is responsible for managing and administering the estate of a deceased person in accordance with the probate rules and procedures of the state in which the probate is taking place. We briefly talked about some of the executor's main responsibilities in Chapter 1, but there are others.

An executor's main responsibilities include the following tasks:

- locating the deceased's last will and testament;

- checking the validity of the last will;

- filing an application for probate with the probate court where the estate does not qualify for an exemption from probate by virtue of it being a small estate (being an estate with a value under a particular threshold, which varies from state to state);

- notifying the beneficiaries named in the deceased's will that he has filed a petition for probate;

- drafting a notice of the deceased's death and arranging publication of that notice in a newspaper;

- notifying known creditors of the deceased that the deceased has passed away and of their entitlement to claim against the deceased's estate;

- sending copies of the deceased's official death notice to the post office, utility companies, banks, credit card companies, etc;

- collecting, securing and inventorying the deceased's assets;

- having the deceased's assets appraised and valued;

- collecting all monies owing to the estate including unpaid salary and other benefits such as social security, civil service, veteran and other benefits;

- filing claims for and collecting the proceeds of life insurance policies payable to the estate;

- filing state death tax and federal estate tax returns;

- paying out valid and proven claims against the estate;

- distributing the remaining assets of the estate to the beneficiaries named in the deceased's will;

- filing all relevant papers with the probate court to wind up the estate; and

- closing probate.

Did You Know?

An executor will be subject to certain laws, regulations, standards and guidelines including (amongst others):

- the terms of the deceased's last will and testament;

- the law of trusts - which is a body of principles adopted by courts over the years which apply to executors and trustees;

- state & federal laws; and

- probate court regulations.

General Duties of an Executor

An executor has a general duty to administer the deceased's estate and to distribute the assets of the estate to the beneficiaries named in the deceased's will or, in the absence of the deceased having made a valid will, to his heirs as determined by state intestacy laws. In carrying out this duty, an executor will be obliged to act promptly and in the best interests of the estate, the creditors, and the deceased's beneficiaries/heirs.

While there is an overlap between the general duties and responsibilities of an executor, the principal duties of an executor include the duty to:

- take possession of the deceased's property;

- manage, protect and preserve the value of the deceased's estate;

- prepare an inventory of all the probatable property owned by the deceased at the time of his death. This inventory should be prepared within a specific time frame (usually three months of the executor's appointment) and should list each item of property together with (i) details of the property's market value at the date of the deceased's death and (ii) details of any encumbrances or security interest registered against that property. Where a market valuation was carried out for a specific item of property, details of the valuation agent used to carry out that valuation should also be included in the inventory;

- publish a creditors' notice. Generally, this notice must be published in a newspaper circulating in the county in which probate has been filed. The notice should be published once a week for three successive weeks and should (i) state that the deceased has died, (ii) include details of the identity of the executor of the deceased's estate and (iii) state that creditors of the deceased's estate can present details of any claims that they might have against the estate to the executor for a period of three months following the date of first publication of the notice. Once this period of time expires, creditors will no longer be able to make a claim against the estate;

- decide which creditors' claims should be allowed and which should be disallowed; and

- pay allowed creditors' claims. Many states prioritize creditors' claims in an order similar to the following:

    (i)   funeral expenses;

    (ii)   costs and expenses associated with the administration of the estate;

    (iii) federal debts and taxes owed by the estate;

    (iv)   medical expenses associated with the final illness of the deceased;

    (v)   state debts and taxes owed by the estate; and

    (vi)   all other creditor claims.

Did You Know?

Duty to prepare an inventory of the deceased's assets

The Uniform Probate Code, which has been adopted by a number of states, requires that, three months after his appointment, an executor must prepare an inventory of the property owned by the deceased at the time of his death. The inventory should include details of the fair market value of each piece of property as at the date of the deceased's death, and the type and amount of any encumbrance that may exist with reference to that property. The executor is obliged to send a copy of the inventory to all interested persons who request it and/or file a copy of the inventory with the probate court. Once filed, the inventory may become a public record.

Fiduciary Duties of an Executor

A fiduciary relationship is a relationship which implies a position of trust or confidence in which one person is entrusted to hold or manage property or money on behalf of another.

Did You Know?

A fiduciary is someone who has undertaken to act for and on behalf of another in a particular matter in circumstances which give rise to a relationship of trust and confidence.

As a fiduciary, the executor owes a number of duties to the creditors and beneficiaries of the deceased's estate. These duties include the duty to:-

- adhere to the terms of the deceased's last will as regards the distribution of his estate;

- locate, take possession of and secure the estate assets;

- keep estate assets separate from other assets – particularly the executor's own assets;

- act personally on behalf of the deceased;

- administer the estate in the best interests of the creditors and the beneficiaries;

- keep accurate records and accounts of all dealings in relation to the estate;

- provide information to creditors, beneficiaries and other persons with a legal interest in the estate in a timely manner;

- administer the estate with the same due care and skill that a person of ordinary prudence would exercise in dealing with his own property; and

- avoid all conflicts of interest.

Duty to Adhere to the Terms of the Will

It is surprising how often executors make decisions without first referring to the deceased's last will and testament to determine whether the act in question is permitted under the terms of the will. A prudent executor will take the time to carefully read the deceased's will in order to understand the scope of the duties assigned to him and to determine what immediate actions he needs to take. A reading of the will should be the first task an executor carries out once receiving or locating the will.

Duty to Secure Assets

As an executor is charged with preserving the value of the deceased's estate, immediately upon his appointment he should seek to locate and secure all of deceased's assets. This duty to secure assets extends to both physically safeguarding and securing assets and also to insuring those assets where prudent to do so.

Duty to Keep Estate Assets Separate from Other Assets

An executor should ensure that (i) the estate assets are kept wholly separate from both his own assets and third party assets, (ii) the title to each estate asset rests exclusively with the estate and not with the executor personally, (iii) he accounts in full to the estate for all income generated by the estate assets and (iv) he does not borrow or otherwise take money from the estate for his own benefit.

Duty to Act Personally

Unless the terms of the will or state law otherwise permit, executors must act personally on behalf of the deceased's estate and may not delegate the performance of any tasks or the making of any decisions concerning the estate to a third party. This does not however restrict the executor's right to obtain legal or other professional advice where he deems it appropriate.

Duty to Act in the Best Interests of the Beneficiaries

An executor is required to act impartially and in the best interests of the estate's creditors and beneficiaries.

Duty to Account

An executor is required to maintain detailed records of all transactions relating to the estate and its assets and, from time to time, to provide a copy of those records to persons who have a legal interest in the estate.. In particular, an executor is obliged to keep detailed records of income generated by the estate's assets, any sale or purchase of estate assets and any payments made using estate assets including all payments of taxes and debts and all distributions made to beneficiaries.

Duty to Exercise Due Care and Invest Prudently

State law provides that an executor must exercise the same due care, diligence and skill in managing the estate assets that would be expected from a prudent person carrying on the same task. This being so, it follows that an executor needs to diversify the estate's investments in order to balance the potential risk of a depletion in the value of those investments. In tandem with doing this, he also needs to ensure the generation of income from the estate assets while at the same time ensuring that the value of those assets grows. For these reasons, it's prudent for an executor (who will often have little investment experience) to engage the services of an investment advisor who can provide investment advice and guidance to him. The appointment of such an advisor becomes more prudent when account is taken of the fact that any failure by the executor to act diligently and prudently in the management of the estate assets could result in the beneficiaries suing him personally for any depletion in the value of the estate assets. However, if the executor acts prudently, it is unlikely that he could be sued even where the value of the estate assets is reduced.

 Important Note

Certain state laws, such as those in Washington, require executors to exercise the same "judgment and care" that a person of ordinary prudence and intelligence would exercise in managing his own affairs. This does not however mean that an executor can take the same risks with the estate assets as he would with his own assets. On the contrary, it means that executors have to be even more prudent when dealing with estate assets.

Duty to Avoid Conflicts of Interest

Executors are required to act in good faith in the best interests of the creditors and beneficiaries of the deceased's estate; and to avoid any conflicts of interest which might cause them to act otherwise. If a conflict of interest does arise, an executor will need to act very carefully and should consider taking professional legal advice before taking any actions.

Even good intentions on the part of the executor are not an acceptable excuse for breaching this duty. Take, for example, a scenario in which an executor is acting on behalf of an estate which has a vast amount of real estate but very little cash with which to pay its outstanding debts and taxes. The executor, believing it would help cash flows for the estate, purchases a piece of real estate from the estate at fair market value. A presumption is immediately raised that, as the executor is self-dealing, he is in breach of his duty to avoid a conflict of interest and act in the best interests of the estate's beneficiaries. As a result, the beneficiaries of the estate file a petition in court challenging the executor's actions. The court, while acknowledging that the executor purchased the property at market value and in good faith, determines that he has in fact breached his duty by not placing the property on the open market and orders that (i) the property be returned by the executor to the estate and (ii) the executor be removed from office.

Important Note

An executor is entitled to engage professionals such as attorneys, accountants and financial advisors to assist him in carrying out his duties and responsibilities. By engaging professionals when needed, an executor can substantially reduce the risk of breaching his fiduciary duties. However, professional advisors should be chosen with care. A list of questions that an executor should ask a professional advisor before formally engaging him is set out below:-

- What licenses, certificates and registrations do you hold?

- What services do you provide?

- What type of clients do you work for?

- How many clients do you have?

- How long have you been in this business?

- What are your educational credentials?

- What is your specific field of expertise?

- How do you keep up to date with changes in your field?

Important Note

- What professional references can you give me?

- Is your performance record verified by independent sources?

- How are your fees calculated?

- Do you have a minimum account fee?

- What exact services will I receive for that fee?

- How often do you communicate with your clients?

Powers of an Executor

Until termination of his appointment, an executor has the same power to deal with the property of the deceased's estate that an absolute owner of that property would have. However, this power is only exercisable by an executor in trust for the benefit of creditors, beneficiaries and others interested in the deceased's estate. This power may be exercised without notice, hearing or order of court.

In addition, executors are also afforded a variety of additional powers under state law. These include powers to:

- employ persons for the purpose of valuing assets and evaluating the liabilities of the estate;

- receive a defined level of compensation or a reasonable level of compensation in return for acting as executor of the estate;

- petition the court for an order determining the validity of a will, the entitlement of beneficiaries to claim under the will, the entitlement of heirs to claim from the estate in the absence of a will, approving the final accounting of the estate as prepared by the executor and the plan of distribution of the estate assets; and

- close the probate or administration of the estate.

As well as the powers granted under state law, executors tend also to be afforded further powers under the terms of a will. These additional powers are given to allow the executor to manage the deceased's estate. Typically, the larger the estate is, the greater the extent of the powers given to the executor. For instance, if the deceased had a large property portfolio and a variety of business interests, he may need to give wide management powers or even a power of sale to the executor in order to ensure that the executor can manage and deal with the estate assets in a manner that ensures that the value of those assets is maintained for the benefit of the beneficiaries.

Executor's Liability

There are numerous risks associated with acting as an executor. Listed below are a number of ways in which an executor could be held liable for a breach of duty or responsibility.

- An executor can be held liable if he:-

    - violates any applicable law;

    - fails to comply with the terms of the will;

    - abuses any of his powers as executor; or

    - deals in the estate assets for his own account or benefit.

- The administration of the estate generally needs to be commenced and concluded within a reasonable period of time. If the executor fails to do this and, as a result, the beneficiaries under the will are exposed to any form of financial loss, he could be held personally liable to the beneficiaries/estate for that loss.

- An executor is obliged to secure and protect the assets of the estate. If he fails to do so and, as a result, the assets are damaged, lost or stolen then (in the absence of having adequate insurance over the assets to cover the loss) he could be held personally liable for any loss or reduction in value of the assets. Similarly, if the executor fails to properly manage, insure or repair real property (whether commercial or residential) he could be held liable for any resulting losses including loss of rental income.

- Executors are required to act prudently in the management of estate assets and investments. If an executor acts without due care and prudence, such as in the case of buying speculative securities or disposing of valuable assets substantially below market value, he could be held accountable.

- While executors can take professional advice before making investment decisions, the authority to make these decisions is personal to the executor and cannot be delegated. Therefore any improper delegation of executor duties, such as allowing investment advisors complete freedom to make decisions in respect of and deal with the estate's investments without executor supervision, could result in liability for the executor. This is true regardless of the assets in question. As such, it would apply equally where the executor allows a third party to freely manage the deceased's business or property portfolio without supervision. If an executor engages a professional to manage any aspect of the estate, the executor most closely supervise the carrying out of those management functions – it is his responsibility after all!

- An executor is responsible for ensuring that the correct people benefit from the estate. If he accidently makes a payment or distribution to the wrong person, he could be held personally liable to make good the damage caused by securing the return of the misplaced assets or compensating the beneficiaries accordingly.

- Taking actions without the proper approval can also expose executors to liability. Depending on the proposed action in question, an executor may require the prior consent of beneficiaries, co-fiduciaries or even a court.

- An executor will always need to ensure that he has properly attended to the payment of all creditor accounts, including any taxation liabilities. An executor will be personally liable to ensure these payments are made where the estate is in funds to meet these payments.

It should be remembered that a beneficiary named under the deceased's will or even a co-executor can institute legal proceedings against the executor for breach of duty or responsibility. The remedies that can be sought by the litigant vary depending on the nature of the alleged breach of duty or responsibility and the specific circumstances involved. However, the principal remedies available would include an order of court:

- compelling the executor to perform his duties;

- preventing the executor from committing a potential violation of his duties;

- requiring the executor to compensate the estate for any violation; and/or

- removing the executor from office.

 Important Note

If you are in any doubt as to your specific duties as executor or if you are concerned as to whether a particular course of action might lead to a breach of duty, we recommend that you seek the advice of an attorney.

Protections for the Executor from Liability

There are a number of ways that an executor can be protected from liability. This protection may be against malfeasance (a term that refers to the committing of an illegal act, especially by a public official) or negligence. While some of these methods need to be provided for under the terms of a will, others can be implemented after the testator's death.

Protection Under the Terms of a Will

The terms of a will can be drafted in a manner so as to reduce the chance of an executor being exposed to personal liability in circumstances where he acts diligently and in good faith in the carrying out of his duties.

By way of simple example, a will could authorize an executor to manage a particular business activity that was somewhat risky and, in conjunction with doing that, could provide that the executor will not be held liable for any loss to the value of that business where he acts in good faith. The rationale for the inclusion of such clauses is relatively straightforward. In the absence of including these exclusion clauses, executors would abstain from taking on any involvement in the management of such assets especially in circumstances where they could find themselves being sued personally for any subsequent loss – even where they did all in their power to prevent the loss. These clauses allow executors to get on with the business at hand while at the same time ensuring that they still act with due care and attention in the performance of their duties.

Obtaining the Consent of Beneficiaries

Another way that executor can reduce the possibility of incurring personal liability is by obtaining the written permission of all concerned beneficiaries before taking a particular course of action such as, for example, selling a particular real estate investment. While it's not vital, the written consent should expressly state that the beneficiaries will not hold the executor liable if he carries out the approved action(s). The mere existence of such a written approval would make it exceptionally difficult for the beneficiaries to subsequently sue the executor for losses to the estate incurred as a result of approved activities having been carried out (unless of course the executor was negligent in carrying out any of the activities approved by the beneficiaries).

Taking Out an Executor's Insurance Bond

One of the best protections available to executors is insurance cover. The estate or the executor can take out executor insurance in the form of a surety bond, obtainable from most insurance companies. The bond protects both the beneficiaries and creditors of the estate from losses suffered as a result of the negligent acts or omissions of the executor. Although a bond is not always required, either the beneficiaries or the probate court may request it from time to time. Needless to say, while it protects the estate, it also protects the executor from personal liability as he is afforded monetary protection up to the value of the insurance bond. The value of the bond should, in most cases, equate to the full value of the estate. The premium for the bond will be payable by the estate.

Obtain the Consent of the Probate Court

Finally, if a particular situation arises during the probate process and an executor is uncertain as to how he should proceed, he can apply to the court for directions as to how he should proceed. Having considered the issue, the court will direct the executor on how best to proceed in the circumstances. This direction will be given in the form of a court order. Where the executor follows the directions of the court order to the letter, it would be extremely difficult for a beneficiary to take action personally against the executor given that he is carrying out actions sanctioned by the court. Of course, if the court was not aware of all the facts in the case, the executor may not be adequately protected in this instance.

Payment of Compensation to Executors

Generally speaking, the amount of compensation payable to executors for carrying out their work ranges from between 2% to 4% of the value of the estate or, in many cases, is limited to 'reasonable compensation'. As the amount which an executor can receive is set out under state law, this amount varies from state to state and also tends to decrease on a percentage basis as the size of the estate increases.

In most cases, however, as executors are often relatives or close friends of the deceased they choose not to charge the estate a fee for taking on the role of executor or carrying out the related duties.

In order for executors to recover fees for the provision of their services or reimbursement for out-of-pocket expenses, they will generally require the prior approval of the probate court. However, in circumstances where the probate court determines that the executor was incompetent or failed to properly carry out his duties and/or responsibilities as executor, the court may deny the payment of compensation to the executor or reduce the amount which ought to be payable to him.

Should You Accept Your Appointment as Executor?

While it's an onerous obligation, the task of being an executor for a family member or a close friend can be seen as a final act of friendship. It's often humbling that someone trusts you sufficiently to invite you to accept this very personal responsibility. In many ways, you should feel honored to have been chosen.

However, having been chosen for this job is not of itself sufficient reason to accept the responsibility especially if you are not 100% committed to the task. In such circumstances, it's much better for everyone if you decline the job when you are originally asked rather than for you to half-heartedly agree to act and then decide you can't do it after the testator's passing.

Assuming however that you're willing in principle at least to carry out the job, there's no reason to refuse to accept the position. If you feel a bit out of your depth at any stage and feel it would be beneficial to the estate for you to do so, you can seek the advice and assistance of an experienced professional — be it a lawyer, accountant or otherwise. Remember, you are entitled to seek professional assistance at the expense of the estate.

All that said, you may very well have good reason for your hesitancy in serving as executor, even for a close friend or family member's estate. Maybe you're in poor health generally? Maybe you are aware of a strong possibility of conflict between certain beneficiaries of the estate which you really don't want to be involved in? Maybe the deceased carried a lot of debt and that concerns you? These sorts of things are all valid reasons for you to hesitate in accepting or even to outright reject the role of executor.

If after taking all of the above into consideration you are still willing to take on the role, remember that the only qualities an executor really cannot do without are conscientiousness, integrity and common sense. Frankly, if you have an organized mind, are reasonably prudent and are detail oriented, there is absolutely no reason for you to have any doubts about serving. Remember you can always seek help from a lawyer or accountant if you need to!

What to Expect When Appointed

If you take on the role of executor, you shouldn't expect all plain sailing when appointed. There are bound to be one or two delays and difficulties in the smoothest of estate administrations. The tardy debtor, the disputatious heir, the accidental or fraudulent claim by a creditor for a debt already paid by the deceased, even the occasional difficulty in tracking down a beneficiary — at least one of these things will be sent to haunt most honest, hard-working executors.

While problems will invariably arise, as executor you will be charged with ensuring that the process is kept moving. To do this, you will need to be aware of the various stages involved in the probate process and what you will need to do at each stage. Be sure, therefore, to read this book carefully and in full if you do accept the role.

Resigning After Accepting the Appointment

While you may have initially felt confident enough to take on the role of executor, you may subsequently discover that there is a lot more involved than you thought. You may even feel that the role is far too demanding both in terms of its time requirement and the strains caused by the complexity of the estate. You may even feel that you've taken on more than you can cope with.

The good news is that you don't have to complete the job even where your appointment has been approved by the probate court. You are free to vacate the office of executor at any time. However, before doing so, there will be some procedural requirements that you must first deal with. If you wish to resign as executor after taking control of the testator's property, you must formally renounce your position in writing. In order to do this, you will need to submit a written letter of renunciation to the probate court. The precise form of this letter varies from state to state. As such, you should check with your local probate court to obtain a copy of the precise form required.

You will also have to provide the court with any information you have already gathered in relation to the deceased's estate. This information will subsequently be passed on to the person who takes on the role of executor following your departure. If there was a second or alternate executor named in the deceased's will, this person will be asked to accept the role upon your resignation. If they are unable or unwilling to accept the role, the court will choose someone to act as executor in the same way as it would choose a person to act as an administrator if there was no will (see Chapter 1).

Important Note

If you have decided to resign, remember to let the immediate relatives of the deceased know of your decision as soon as possible so that they can promptly deal with the appointment of a new executor/administrator.

Declining to Act as Executor

While a testator should always enquire as to whether a person would be willing to act as an executor before naming that person in his will, the reality is that the task is sometimes sprung on the person completely out of the blue. If you have been nominated as executor and are unwilling to take on the role, you are free to decline to act at any time. By this we mean that you can not only say "no" when you are initially asked to act as executor, but you can also decide on the death of the testator that you do not want to take on the role of executor - even where you have previously agreed to accept the role and have been expressly nominated in the will. For instance, you may have come to the decision that it's just too much trouble and responsibility. And that's perfectly fine. It's only after the filing of the petition for probate in the probate court that your right to resign is restricted (see above).

An executor's job is often not an easy one, especially where the affairs of the deceased were not in order at the time of his death and/or where the deceased owed a lot of money at the time of his death. Obviously, the more assets and liabilities that the deceased had the longer it will take to wind up their estate. These potential complications and delays alone are often enough to encourage would be executors to turn down the role.

Probate can be a long drawn out and demanding process even with the assistance of an experienced probate lawyer. If the estate is complex, you may not be comfortable with your ability to carry out your duties or may even be worried about potential exposure to liability. If, at the end of the day, you feel (for whatever reason) that you would be unable for the job, then you should not accept the position. This would undoubtedly be the best for everyone.

You should note that even where you decline to act as executor you are legally required to file the deceased's will with the deceased's local probate court if you are in possession of it at the time of the deceased's death. There are specific time lines within which the will must be presented to the probate court – often within 30 days of its discovery. You should check your state laws or with the local probate court to determine the precise requirements in this respect.

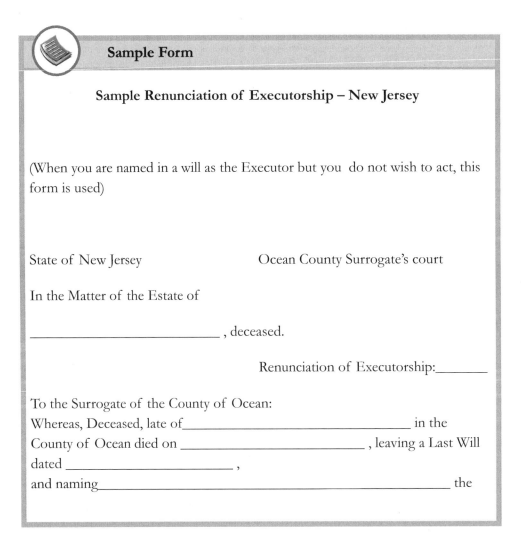

Sample Form

Sample Renunciation of Executorship – New Jersey

(When you are named in a will as the Executor but you do not wish to act, this form is used)

State of New Jersey   Ocean County Surrogate's court

In the Matter of the Estate of

_____ , deceased.

Renunciation of Executorship:_____

To the Surrogate of the County of Ocean:
Whereas, Deceased, late of_____ in the
County of Ocean died on _____ , leaving a Last Will
dated _____ ,
and naming_____ the

Executor/rix thereof.

Now be it known that _____

_____ hereby renounces the said executorship and refuses to take upon himself/herself the burden of the same.

_____

Signed in the presence of

_____

Notary Public

STATE OF NEW JERSEY

COUNTY OF   ss:

Be it Remembered, that on _____ before me, the undersigned authority personally appeared _____

_____ who I am satisfied is the person in the foregoing instrument named, to whom I first made known the contents thereof, he/she did thereupon acknowledge that he/she signed, sealed and delivered the same as his/her act and deed, for the uses and purposes therein expressed.

                              _____

                              AFFIX SEAL   Notary Public

CHAPTER 3:

EXECUTOR'S DUTIES: WHAT TO DO IMMEDIATELY AFTER DEATH

Chapter Overview

In this chapter, we look at some of the more common tasks that an executor might need to deal with immediately following the death of the testator.

Chapter

3

CHAPTER 3

EXECUTOR'S DUTIES: WHAT TO DO IMMEDIATELY AFTER DEATH

Introduction

The death of a loved one often has a huge emotional impact on the surviving family and friends of the deceased. Notwithstanding these emotional difficulties, there will be a number of tasks that the deceased's family will need to tend to immediately following the deceased's death. The most important of these tasks include (i) organizing organ donations, (ii) making funeral arrangements and (iii) making burial arrangements. We take a detailed look at these and other tasks over the ensuing pages.

What to Do If Death Occurs at Home

Death at home is quite a common occurrence. In many cases, it's planned. In other cases, however, it's completely unexpected and takes the deceased's family by surprise. When death does occur, there will be a number of tasks that need attending to without undue delay. These tasks include the following:-

- the deceased's family doctor will need to be contacted and asked to come to the deceased's home in order to pronounce death;

- if the deceased wanted to donate any of his organs, the deceased's family doctor and/or the donee organization should be contacted immediately following the deceased's death. As a general rule, the deceased's organs will only be suitable for donation if they are extracted from the deceased within a specific time frame following his death. In many cases, where death occurs at home rather than in a medical care facility, the organs will not be capable of being extracted in time;

- the nearest relatives of the deceased will need to be contacted and informed of the death, as will certain close friends and colleagues of the deceased;

- if the death occurred in unusual circumstances, the police will need to be called;

- if the deceased was religious, the relevant minister of religion will need to be contacted;

- an undertaker will need to be contacted in order to arrange for the laying out and transporting of the deceased's body; and

- the deceased's last will and testament will need to be located as would any letter of instruction setting out details of the deceased's funeral requirements/requests.

In your capacity as a nominated executor and/or family member or friend of the deceased, you should be able to assist the deceased's family with each of the above tasks during this difficult period.

Autopsy Requirements

Autopsies are required by law to determine the cause of death in cases of violent death and death by unknown circumstances. It consists of a simple systematic examination of the body by a pathologist for the purpose of determining the cause of death.

Happily an autopsy is not usually needed in the case of a natural death as there is generally enough information available from the attending physician to satisfactorily determine the cause of death. However, if satisfactory medical information is unavailable or if circumstances require, an autopsy will need to be performed to determine the cause of death. In such circumstances, an autopsy will be conducted irrespective of the views of the deceased's family, friends and others.

If the deceased had religious beliefs prohibiting an autopsy and either you (as potential executor) or the deceased's family are in possession of a certified letter documenting the deceased's wish that no autopsy be performed, this letter should be supplied to the coroner's office as soon as possible following the deceased's death. Most coroners' offices will make every effort possible to honor the deceased's wishes in this respect.

Organize Anatomic Gifts

If the testator has made you aware of his intentions to make an organ or body donation on his death, it's important to ensure that steps are taken prior to his death to ensure that his wishes can be honored when the time comes. In this regard, it will be important to have the testator complete a donor card and to know the location of that card. It will also be important to ensure that the testator's family are on board with the testator's wishes and that appropriate arrangements are made in advance to ensure the speedy delivery of the testator's organs and/or body to the donee on his death.

Important Note

Donor cards (also called gift cards, gift documents and anatomical gift cards) contain details of the donor's wishes in relation to the making of anatomical gifts following his death. It is important that these cards are used and that details of the testator's wishes are not simply set out in his will. If this happens, there will be a risk that the donor's will remains unread for several days following his death and that any opportunity to make an anatomical gift will have been missed. Best practice is to include the wishes on a donor card, in the donor's last will and in the donor's letter of instruction.

Under the Uniform Anatomical Gift Act, which is currently the law in all states, any gifts of organs or of the entire body made in writing by the deceased must be honored by his survivors irrespective of whether they agree with them or not. However, as delay in transporting the organs and/or body to the new recipient is the main reason why donations are rejected, it's important that the family is on side to ensure the prompt transfer of the body or organs. If the body or organs are not received by the donee within a few hours of the deceased's death, they will be rejected. As such, time is very much of the essence.

If testator's survivors are unable to transport the body or organs in time to the donee or if the donation is rejected for any other reason, the deceased's family is free to choose any alternative method of body/organ disposal they wish.

As an executor, you may need to familiarize yourself with state laws governing anatomic gifts and/or autopsies as those laws may well stipulate who has the final say in relation to the making of funeral arrangements, the disposal of the body and the responsibility for the funeral bill where the anatomic gift is not accepted. While these laws are often innocently violated by families caught up in grief, an understanding of these laws may help you avert any potential problems in this respect before they arise.

Obtain Copies of the Death Certificate

A death certificate should be obtained as soon as possible following the deceased's death. The certificate can usually be obtained from the state offices of vital records or the department of health - but there are some variations in these office names from state to state. Alternatively, the deceased's general practitioner should be able to obtain a copy of the certificate.

As mentioned in the previous section, where it is unclear as to how the deceased actually died, it may become necessary for the hospital where the deceased died (or, where the death was at home, the general practitioner who attended to the deceased) to notify the coroner with a view to having an autopsy carried out. Where this happens, the death certificate will not be available until after the coroner completes his examination of the deceased.

Once the death certificate has been obtained, the deceased can be formally released into the care of a funeral director who, in turn, can begin to make funeral arrangements in conjunction with the deceased's family. More importantly for executors, the release of the death certificate signifies the commencement of the period in which probate can be initiated. Of course, most executors will wait until a short time after the deceased has been buried or cremated before commencing probate. In fact, the law in many states will require a certain number of days to have passed before a probate proceeding can begin.

In order for an executor to wind up the deceased's estate he will need to obtain a certified copy (or preferably, for ease, multiple certified copies) of the death certificate. This is needed to transfer ownership of or sell real estate, stock certificates, motor vehicles, etc, to beneficiaries or third parties and to collect the benefits payable to the deceased's estate under any insurance policies.

Certified copies of the death certificate will also be required to access any safe deposit boxes held by the deceased at the time of his death. In addition, financial institutions such as banks and life insurance companies will usually require a certified copy of the death certificate before allowing executors access the accounts and funds of a deceased customer. For this reason, you may wish to order 4-6 copies of the death certificate.

Review Letter of Instruction

If you have agreed to become an executor for a testator who is still alive, you should encourage him to complete a letter of instruction. A letter of instruction is a document which gives the testator's family and executor timely, private and useful information concerning the administration of his estate and related matters.

A letter of instruction is guaranteed to ease the burden on the surviving members of the deceased's family by giving them concise and specific information regarding the deceased's assets and liabilities. It also has the benefit of significantly reducing the possibility that some of the deceased's assets will go undiscovered following his death. The deceased's family members will invariably be extremely grateful for the testator's thoughtfulness and foresight in preparing such a letter - as indeed will any executor who has encouraged him to do so.

As letters of instruction are unique to the assets, liabilities and dealings of each author, a one-fits-all template cannot be easily created. That said, set out below are details of the matters that are most often included in letters of instruction. However, before a testator makes any decisions as to which of these matters he would like to include in his letter, he will first need to give some careful consideration as to who will receive copies of the letter before his death and whether or not it is appropriate to alert those recipients to certain matters relating to his private affairs. Of course, if there are some sensitive issues, the testator may wish to prepare more than one version of the letter – one for his family generally and perhaps one for his executor's eyes only.

In the example below we have split the letter of instruction into six separate parts namely (i) Emergency Information, (ii) Available Money & Sources of Income & Pensions (iii) Investments & Securities, (iv) Real Estate, (v) Business & Professional Interests and (vi) Miscellaneous. The list below is by no means an exhaustive list, but it's certainly a start!

(For ease of description, we have used the title "testator" to describe the person who is writing the letter of instruction.)

Letter of Instruction

(i) Emergency Information

The following emergency information should be included in the testator's letter of instruction:-

- organ donation preferences – in addition to noting the organs to be donated, the recipient organization needs to be noted along with a contact telephone number that will enable the testator's family to arrange the donations promptly upon the testator's death. This is important as the post-mortem medical procedures need to be done promptly following death;

- where the original and latest version of the testator's last will and testament is located;

- autopsy preferences – any significant personal preferences regarding autopsies should be stated, together with the reasons for such preferences. That way, the testator's views can be taken into consideration by the coroner when the time comes – subject to state legal requirements of course;

- funeral and interment preferences – the testator should express his wishes in relation to these matters clearly and concisely. For example, he should clearly set out his wishes for (a) cremation or burial, (b) preferred place of burial or what he wants done with his ashes, (c) religious or secular services, and (d) who should be notified of the testator's death when the time comes. In the context of funeral arrangements, it's often better for the testator to have a proper funeral plan prepared. In this regard, reference should be made to Enodare's book "Funeral Planning Basics" which details all of the various options associated with funeral planning, the cost of those options and how to make a customized personal funeral plan;

- obituary requirements – the preparation of obituaries and eulogies can be very traumatic and difficult tasks. As such, it can be useful to have the testator write down a few points about what he would like included and, depending on the circumstances, perhaps even prepare a rough draft;

- child care – guidelines and instructions to the person tasked with caring for the testator's children after his death (the nomination of this caregiver, known as the guardian, should be in the testator's will) ; and

- animal care – who should be responsible for looking after the testator's animals following his death. This can also be specified in the testator's will.

(ii) Available Money, Sources of Income & Pensions

Details of:-

- checking accounts;

- savings accounts;

- debit and credit cards;

- certificates of deposit;

- employment income – full, part-time and/or independent income;

- alimony payments;

- child support payments;

- workers' compensation;

- rental income;

- royalties receivable;

- dividends receivable;

- interest receivable;

- military pension;

- union pension;

- 401(K) plan;

- retirement account; and

- miscellaneous sources of income.

(iii) Investments & Securities

Details of:-

- stocks;

- bonds;

- futures;

- and options.

(iv) Real Estate

Details of:-

- family home;

- vacation home(s);

- rental properties & lease/tenant details;

- timeshare interests; and

- land holdings.

(v) Business & Professional Interests

Details of:-

- sole proprietorships;

- partnership interests;

- shares in companies;

- miscellaneous business interests;

- intellectual property rights; and

- royalties.

(vi) Miscellaneous Items

Details of:-

- personal information;

- location of personal documents;

- location of personal assets;

- location of safe deposit boxes and details on how to access them;

- existence of debts;

- medical information;

- death and funeral plans;

- PIN numbers and passwords;

- address book; and

- professional and other advisors.

The task of preparing a letter of instruction can be a time consuming process, but once done, the testator will have a template that he can simply add to or subtract from whenever necessary – without the need to completely redo the document every time.

Locate the Will and Other Important Papers

Locating the deceased's last will and testament can often be a difficult task. Ideally, the deceased should have made his chosen executor or family members aware of its location. However, quite often there will be somewhat of a 'fishing expedition' for the document following the deceased's death. If it cannot be found with the deceased's personal papers and possessions, it's a good idea to check with the county probate court. A large number of people file their wills at the local court for safekeeping. Another very likely place to find the will is at the office of the deceased's lawyer – especially if that lawyer prepared the will on behalf of the deceased.

If the deceased's original will cannot be found, the laws in a number of states allow for a photocopy of the deceased's will to be admitted to probate in place of the original document. You will need to check the laws of the state in which the probate is taking place to find out the appropriate procedure for proving a lost will or copy will. Many states allow for the copy wills to be admitted to probate where witnesses can verify that the original of the copy will was in fact signed by the testator and properly executed.

Did You Know?

Once a will has been admitted to probate, it is placed on the public record and will be made available to anyone who wants to see it upon payment of a small fee.

Arrange Funeral and/or Memorial Service

A situation that continually causes friction and resentment within families is the question of who has the right to decide on the funeral arrangements to be made for the deceased and how his body is to be disposed of. Conflicts more often than not arise from generational differences. Take the case, for example, of a young husband who dies and whose wife prefers a simple secular service followed by a cremation. Her preferences are pitched directly against his parents who want an elaborate (and expensive) religious service, an expensive casket, grave burial and a very expensive marker. Who has the last say – the deceased's spouse or parents?

The laws in most states set out details of the people who are legally entitled to make funeral and disposal decisions on behalf of a deceased person. They even set out the order of priority in which the relevant people can make those decisions. While the specific order varies from state to state, it generally takes the following order:

- surviving spouse;

- adult children;

- parent;

- adult sibling;

- guardian; and

- creditors.

While it will not be the responsibility of an executor to arrange the deceased's funeral, the executor will be responsible for ensuring that the costs of the funeral are later discharged from the estate assets. In certain cases, a funeral director may require someone to personally guarantee the payment of funeral expenses if he doesn't know the deceased or if there is a legitimate concern as to whether the estate will discharge the funeral expenses. There is no obligation on the part of the executor to give this guarantee. However, if he feels that the estate can easily make the payment, he may be somewhat relaxed about giving the guarantee. The risk in doing this is that if the estate is unable to make the payment, due to insufficiency of funds, the executor cold be held personally liable for the debt. As an executor, you therefore need to be very careful when providing these types of guarantees.

Even though an executor will not be responsible for making funeral arrangements for the deceased, he should be aware of the arrangements that are being made so that he can keep a careful eye on the costs being incurred and ensure that the deceased's family are not taken advantage of during a very emotional time in their lives. If the executor feels that the funeral costs are excessive, he can (once formally appointed) petition the probate court to have the fees reviewed. Where the probate court forms the view that the deceased's family has been overcharged, it can order that the funeral provider's fees are either reduced or negated in full.

 Resource!

Funeral Planning Basics shows you how to effortlessly plan a funeral. You'll learn about purchasing caskets and grave plots, burial and cremation options, organizing funeral services and much more.

For more information on **Funeral Planning Basics,** visit www.enodare. com.

CHAPTER 4:

MAKING SENSE OF THE WILL AND WHAT TO DO IF THERE ISN'T ONE

Chapter Overview

In this chapter, we take a closer look at wills, what makes them valid and what happens to a person's property if they die without a valid will.

Chapter 4

CHAPTER 4

MAKING SENSE OF THE WILL AND WHAT TO DO IF THERE ISN'T ONE!

Did You Know?

A will or last will & testament is a legal declaration by which a person, known as the testator, names one or more persons to manage his/her estate and provides for the transfer of his property at death.

Determining Whether a Will is Valid

Assuming that you've now located the testator's will, the next step is for you to determine whether or not it appears to be valid. Final determination as to the validity of a will rests with the probate court, but the executor can prevent unnecessary delay by analyzing the likelihood a court will consider a purported will to be valid.

In general, in order for a will to be valid, it must:

- be made by a person who has reached the age of majority in his state (there are certain exceptions to this general rule – see below);

- be made voluntarily and without pressure from any other person. For this reason, it is not advisable for a potential beneficiary to be present when a testator instructs a lawyer to draw up his will;

- be made by someone who is of 'sound and disposing mind';

- be in writing;

- be signed by the testator in the presence of two witnesses (or three witnesses in the state of Vermont);

- be signed by the witnesses, in the presence of the testator, after he has signed it. A beneficiary or their spouse should not be a witness to the signing of the will. If a witness is a beneficiary (or the spouse or registered partner of a beneficiary), the will is still valid but there can be additional challenges to the will's validity, especially as to the validity of the witnesses' share under the will;

- include an attestation clause. This is a clause which simply explains how the will has been signed and witnessed; and

- in Louisiana, be notarized.

Some states that recognize "holographic" wills do not require that the will be witnessed or notarized. A holographic will is one that is entirely in the testator's own handwriting.

Important Note

While it is important to have a will, not everyone gets around to making one. However, just making a will is not enough. The testator must ensure that the will is valid and that it provides clear instructions to the executors and trustees regarding the management and distribution of his estate.

So, what happens if there is no will? Well, in a manner of speaking, there is no such thing as someone dying without a will. If a person dies without making a will of their own, the state will enforce a substitute will on them (or more to the point on their estate) with pre-defined rules in relation to the distribution of their estate.

Age of Majority

In order to create a valid will, every state requires that the testator must have reached the age of eighteen years. In some states, an emancipated minor may be qualified to make a will even though he or she is not yet eighteen.

In some instances, a court can appoint a conservator or other representative to make a will for someone who is still a minor. This might be approved, for example, where a person under 18 years of age inherited a large amount of money, invented some innovative computer software or created the next Facebook with some friends. In each case, if the minor was shown to be of a disposing capability and the move was deemed prudent, the court might well grant approval for the making of a will in the circumstances

Mental Capacity

The definition of "sound mind" varies from state to state. Typically, the testator must have been of sound and disposing mind and memory when he made his will in order for it to be valid. In other words, the testator needed to have understood:

- what a will was;

- that he was actually making his will;

- the general extent of his property;

- who his relatives and potential heirs were; and

- the manner in which his will proposed to distribute his property (and be satisfied with that!).

If the testator suffered from any kind of mental disorder such as dementia or Alzheimer's disease, or from an addiction to drugs or alcohol; the mental state analyzed is the mental state at the time the testator made his will. For example, suppose the testator developed dementia fifty years after making his will, the court would look fifty years back to evaluate the testator's mental state at the time the will was made. Similarly, if the testator suffered from drug or alcohol addiction but was not under the influence when he signed the will, he will be deemed to have been competent when executing the will (assuming that there was not some other underlying medical condition).

Similar to the rules for minors, a court can appoint a conservator or other representative to make a will for someone who might lack mental capacity.

Undue Influence

Another form of mental incapacity is undue influence. Undue influence is the exertion by a person in a position of trust or authority of any kind of control or influence over another person such that the person signs a contract or other instrument which he or she would not have signed without the influence of the other party. A contract or instrument may be set aside as not binding on any party who signs it while under undue influence. This claim is often raised by sibling beneficiaries where one sibling is bequeathed more under the terms of a will than the others.

Where a testator uses a beneficiary's attorney to draft a will it can create a presumption of undue influence. This presumption can be overcome with proper evidence, but that is one reason the testator should get independent legal advice when making a will.

Format of a Will

While all states recognize the validity of written wills, certain states will not recognize oral or holographic wills. As such, it's important to ensure that the will is in writing, and complies with the laws of the testator's state of residence.

Signing of a Will

Wills ordinarily need to be signed (save where it's an oral will – which is recognized in some states). Typically, the testator can either sign his own will or direct someone to do so on his behalf. Signatures may include marks, initials, a rubber stamp, a 'nick-name', or a former name.

Witnessing a Will

While each state has its own laws setting out how the execution of a will should be witnessed these tend to be quite similar from state to state. Generally speaking, in order for a will to be valid, the testator needs to have signed his name to the will in the presence of two or, in the case of Vermont, three witnesses. In turn, the witnesses should sign their names in the presence of the testator and in the presence of each other.

Notarizing a Will

Only in the state of Louisiana must a non-holographic ("olographic" in Louisiana) will be notarized. In all other states notarization is not required — however it is recommended. With notarization, each of the witnesses sign a document called a 'self-proving affidavit'. This is an affidavit sworn by the witnesses which eliminates the need for them to later testify in front of a probate court that they witnessed the testator signing the will. This affidavit must be sworn before a notary public.

Reading of the Will

Unlike the scene often played out in books and movies, there is no requirement for an official "reading of the will" in front of the heirs or beneficiaries. However, as executor you should read the will as soon as possible following the death of the testator. Where possible, you should only read the original signed version of the will rather than a copy. Copies run the risk of being incomplete, inaccurate and, in some cases, invalid due to revocation (this is where the will has been cancelled by the creation of a later will or the destruction of the original).

Although more and more wills these days are written in clear modern language a good number are still written in an old fashioned legalistic style. As such, it's important to take your time and read the will thoroughly. You may not understand all the legal jargon the first time round, so don't be hesitant about re-reading the will until you are satisfied that you fully understand it. If there are any terms that you do not understand, look them up in your local library or from a valid and reliable source on the internet. If you are still in doubt, pick up the phone and speak to an attorney. It's important that you understand the provisions of the will as this will make things a lot easier for you when it comes to distributing the estate.

Also, in general, the reading of a will can provide you with a good deal of information regarding the testator and his estate, including details of his children, heirs, assets, liabilities, funeral preferences, anatomic gift preferences and so on.

Notifying Beneficiaries and Others

Once you determine that a will is valid, you should notify the parties who will have an interest in the testator's estate under the terms of the will of that entitlement. Where a beneficiary under the will is a minor, you will need to notify the child's parents or guardian. Often wills identify who this is. If a beneficiary is mentally incompetent, you should notify their custodian or conservator. Typically, the parties who need to be notified include:

- beneficiaries and alternate beneficiaries under the will;

- heirs-at-law – even where they do not appear to be entitled under the will; and

- the spouse and the children, if any, of the deceased.

Important Task

Duty to inform heirs and beneficiaries under the probate code

Not later than 30 days after his appointment, every executor must give notice of that appointment to the beneficiaries named in the deceased's will and to certain other heirs. The notice should be delivered or sent by ordinary mail to each of those beneficiaries and heirs and should:

(i)   state the name and address of the executor;

(ii)   state that the notice is being sent to everyone who has or may have an interest in the deceased's estate;

(iii)   indicate whether an executor's bond has been filed with the probate court;

(iv)   include details of the court in which papers relating to the probate of the deceased's estate have been and/or will be filed;

(v)   include details of the state in which the probate proceedings are taking place;

(vi)   state whether the probate is taking place under the supervision of the court;

(vii)   state that all recipients of the notice are entitled to be provided with certain information relating to the probate of the deceased's estate; and

(viii) state that the recipients of the notice are entitled to petition the court in relation to any matters concerning the probate of the deceased's estate including in relation to the distribution of the estate assets and the expenses of administration.

The executor's failure to include any of the required information in the notice is a breach of duty but will not affect the validity of his appointment as an executor.

Dying Intestate

When a person dies without a valid will or if a will cannot be located, is deemed false or invalid for not meeting statutory elements, the person is said to have died intestate. However, even where a person has not actually made their own will, they will still be deemed, in a manner of speaking, to have a will – it's just that the will is a state imposed 'alternative will' derived from the rules of intestate succession. The terms of this will depend on the intestacy laws of the state in which the deceased was resident at the time he died.

 Did You Know?

Over 2.4 million Americans die every year (Source: National Vital Statistics Report). Of this number, research indicates that almost 55% die without having made any form of will. Worse still, of the 45% of people that have actually made a will, 12% of that group will have made wills that, for some reason or another, turn out to be invalid. As a result, the percentage of Americans dying each year without a valid will is approximately 67%.

This 'alternative will', or rules of intestacy as they are properly called, specifies how the estate will be administered and just who is entitled to receive a gift or inheritance from that estate. In some cases, of course, the 'state imposed will' reflects exactly what the deceased would have wanted anyway, but in most cases it does not.

State probate laws determine matters such as:

- who will be entitled to be appointed as administrator of the deceased's estate – a person who will have similar duties and responsibilities to an executor of the estate;

- who will be entitled to be appointed as guardian of the deceased's minor children;

- the powers that will be granted to the administrator and the rules under which he/she must be bonded; and

- who will be entitled to inherit the deceased's estate – such beneficiaries being referred to as "heirs-at-law".

Where a person dies intestate, the intestacy laws of the state in which he was resident at the time of death will determine how his estate is to be distributed amongst his heirs-at-law. Generally, the rule of thumb here is that the first in line to benefit is the surviving spouse and then the children of the deceased. However, if there is no surviving spouse or children, then the general rule of thumb is 'the bigger the estate, the more — and more distant — the relatives who get to share in it.'

The Main Differences Between Dying "Testate" and "Intestate"?	
Testate	**Intestate**
There is a valid will.	There is no will, or the will is invalid.
The will has been signed by the testator.	There is no will, or the will is invalid.
The estate of the deceased is referred to as a "testate" estate.	The estate of the deceased is referred to as an "intestate" estate.
The person dealing with the winding up of the estate will be known as the "executor of the will" or as the "personal representative".	The person dealing with the winding up of the estate will be known as the "administrator of the estate" or the "personal representative".
The personal representative will need to file a petition for probate of a will & letters of authority.	The administrator will need to file a petition for letters of administration.
The person named in the will usually acts as executor or personal representative.	The administrator will be appointed in accordance with the rules of priority set out under state probate law.
The people who receive gifts under a will are called "beneficiaries" or "devisees".	The people who receive distributions on intestacy are called "heirs" or "heirs-at-law".

The Main Differences Between Dying "Testate" and "Intestate"?	
The beneficiaries are named in the will.	The heirs are determined in accordance with the rules of priority set out under state probate law.

Partial Intestacy

In addition to providing for situations where a person has died without making a will, intestacy laws also apply to situations where the testator has failed to deal with all of his property under the terms of his will. This is called a partial intestacy.

Partial intestacy commonly occurs where a will fails to include what's known as a residuary clause. A residuary clause is a clause which provides that any of the deceased's property which has not been specifically gifted to someone under the terms of the will shall be given to a named beneficiary or beneficiaries known as the residuary beneficiary/beneficiaries. A partial intestacy can also occur where the residuary beneficiary or beneficiaries die before the testator and no alternate beneficiaries are named to receive the residue of the estate in their place.

 Did You Know?

A partial intestacy occurs where a testator fails to dispose of his entire estate under his will. In such cases, property not specifically disposed of under the will generally becomes the subject of intestate administration proceedings.

Appointment of an Administrator

The term administrator is the name given to the person appointed to administer an intestate estate (an estate where no will exists, or where none can be found). The deceased's close relatives usually have the highest priority for appointment by the court as administrator. It follows that if the person at the top of the priority list declines then the next person down the list is asked to do the job.

But, if no member of the family is willing to serve, a creditor may apply to the court (naturally because he wishes the estate to pay his claim quickly) for appointment as administrator. Any such petition is only granted after all the heirs have been duly notified of their entitlement to act and have declined to do so.

While the entitlement of persons to be appointed as administrators of a deceased person's estate varies from state to state, it generally goes in the following order:

- surviving spouse or domestic partner;

- children;

- grandchildren;

- other descendents;

- parents;

- brothers and sisters;

- descendents of brothers and sisters;

- grandparents;

- descendents of grandparents;

- children of a predeceased spouse or domestic partner;

- other descendents of a predeceased spouse or domestic partner;

- other next of kin;

- parents of a predeceased spouse or domestic partner;

- descendents of parents of a predeceased spouse or domestic partner;

- conservator or guardian of the estate acting in that capacity at the time of death who has filed a first account and is not acting as conservator or guardian for any other person;

- public administrator;

- creditors; or

- any other suitable person.

If there is an intestacy or a partial intestacy, be sure to check the state intestacy laws of the deceased's state of residence to determine who exactly can be lawfully appointed as administrator. Also, certain states impose time limits on how long the rules of priority apply. Once these time limits expire, which in some cases can occur within 40 days or less following the deceased's passing, any 'suitable person' can apply to the court to be appointed as administrator of the deceased's estate.

Distribution of Assets on Intestacy

While intestacy laws generally vary from state to state, this variance has been greatly lessened by the Uniform Probate Code (the "**Code**") which, at the time of this writing, has been adopted by 18 states in full and by numerous states in part. The Code is a good place to begin a general discussion on this topic. However, you should check state law in the testator's state of residence for a more sophisticated and thorough understanding of the probate code applicable in that state.

UNIFORM PROBATE CODE - FULL STATE ADOPTIONS		
Alaska	Michigan	North Dakota
Arizona	Minnesota	Pennsylvania
Colorado	Montana	South Carolina
Hawaii	Nebraska	South Dakota
Idaho	New Jersey	Utah
Maine	New Mexico	Wisconsin

The Code provides that priority of inheritance is given to the following persons in the following order:

- surviving spouse; descendents (children, grandchildren, etc.);

- parents;

- descendents of deceased's parents (siblings, nieces and nephews);

- grandparents; and

- descendents of grandparents (aunts, uncles and cousins).

Under the Code, relatives are each apportioned a certain percentage of the deceased's estate. The percentages are as follows:

Share of Surviving Spouse

The share of a surviving spouse is calculated as follows:-

- A surviving spouse is entitled to the entire estate if neither the deceased's descendants (i.e. children, grandchildren and great grandchildren) nor the deceased's parents have survived the deceased.

- If the deceased's parents survive but no descendents survive the deceased, the surviving spouse is entitled to the first $200,000 of the estate plus ¾ of anything exceeding that amount.

- If the deceased is survived by a spouse and descendants from that marriage only, the surviving spouse will take the first $150,000 of the estate plus ½ of anything exceeding that amount, plus all community property.

- If the deceased is survived by descendents from the marriage to the surviving spouse and by descendents from someone other than his surviving spouse, the surviving spouse takes the first $100,000 of the estate plus ½ of anything exceeding that amount, plus all community property.

Share of Descendents

- If the deceased's spouse does not survive the deceased and the deceased's descendants do, then the descendents take the entire estate.

- In some cases, if the deceased's child has predeceased the deceased, that child's surviving children will inherit their parent's share of the intestate estate. This is known as 'per stirpes' distribution.

Share of Parents

- If the deceased is not survived by a spouse or descendents, his entire net estate passes to his parents equally or, if only one survives, to the survivor.

Share of Other Relatives

- If neither the deceased's spouse, descendents, nor parents survive the deceased, the entire net estate passes to the deceased's siblings. If there are no siblings or no descendents of the deceased's siblings, the deceased's estate goes to any surviving grandparents or their descendents. Even with all these intestacy provisions, if the deceased dies without a will and without traceable relatives or relatives that fall within the scope of the Code or state intestacy provisions, the ultimate successor will be the state treasury.

Important Note

The administrator of the intestate estate is required to exercise great diligence in identifying and locating the 'heirs-at-law'. To this end, depending on state law, he may need to place advertisements in the newspapers and, if appropriate, engage the services of a genealogist.

Resource!

For more specific information and an intestacy estate calculator please visit www.mystatewill.com/specific_states.htm.

CHAPTER 5:

EXECUTOR DUTIES: TAKING STOCK

Chapter Overview

In this chapter, we look at some of the steps that you should take during the first few weeks following the death of the deceased. In particular, we look at how you can provide for the immediate needs of the deceased's family and at some of the preliminary steps which you could take to protect the value of the deceased's estate.

Chapter 5

CHAPTER 5

EXECUTOR DUTIES: TAKING STOCK

Estimate Cash Needed for Immediate Future

Generally speaking, more often than not the most immediate concern for
dependents when a loved one passes away is the availability of funds to cover
the funeral expenses and to discharge ordinary day-to-day living expenses such
as mortgage payments, educational fees, utility bills, grocery bills and so on.

Given the trauma which the family of the deceased is most likely going through
immediately following the deceased's death, they are often too emotionally
distraught to deal with financial matters. As an executor, you can provide
invaluable assistance to the deceased's family at that particular point in time by
organizing funds to meet their urgent and ongoing needs.

Remember, during the probate process, the majority of the deceased's assets will
be frozen until the letters of authority issue (this is the document that legally
allows the executor to deal with the assets of the deceased). As such, you will
need to consider how best to procure funds to meet the family's immediate
needs. You can usually do this in one of two ways.

Firstly, many financial institutions offer loans to heirs and beneficiaries who
are waiting to receive inheritances. In many cases, assuming that the beneficiary
meets the financial requirements of the bank in question, money can be
advanced in as little as 72 hours. However, it's important to read the small print.
Unlike a standard loan, many of these financial institutions take an assignment
of the beneficiary's right to receive an element or amount of their inheritance.
As there are often no periodical loan repayments or interest repayments on
this loan, the amount assigned includes a premium for putting the facility in
place. This premium can be exceptionally high in cases so beware. All that said,

it should be possible to secure a fairly standard loan with standard repayment obligations from a regular bank if needed.

The second and better way for the family of the deceased to get their hands on funds derives from the fact that not all assets need to go through probate; and as such are not frozen pending completion of the probate process. These assets include items such as insurance proceeds, assets held in a living trust, joint bank accounts, property held in joint tenancy or assets passing to a designated beneficiary on death. While there is a detailed discussion on assets that don't go through probate in Chapter 7, suffice to say for the moment that these assets can provide an immediate lifeline to the family and can often be accessed with just the death certificate of the deceased. However, be realistic in your expectations as extracting the proceeds payable under a life policy, for example, may take a number of weeks or even months notwithstanding that there may be a beneficiary designated under the policy itself.

With the family's consent and the consent of all beneficiaries under the will, you could also consider selling some of the deceased's personal property (which is not normally frozen by probate) in order to raise money. For example, you could sell furniture, cars, collectibles, etc. However, keep in mind that your authority to sell assets does not actually begin until letters of authority are issued, so you want to be sure to have the permission of all of the beneficiaries before selling anything before that time.

The state also does its bit in providing for the needs of a surviving spouse and minor children by providing 'financial assistance' for the surviving spouse as well as the deceased's minor children. This financial assistance comes in the form of "homestead rights". This is a right given to the deceased's family to remain in and occupy the deceased's home for a period of time — even in the case where the home has been left to someone else. However, while the state does its bit, it's too often insufficient to provide for the needs of the deceased's family throughout the entire probate process. As such, you should consider all options available to the family in order to facilitate them through the entire probate process — which can go on for over a year in some cases!

Unfortunately, however, there are often occasions when no funds are immediately available. What do you do if the banks are unwilling to make arrangements to help the survivors out? Well, you may have to use your position as executor to arrange a loan for the deceased's family until the assets of the estate are released and distributed. In most cases, executors will be able to take out a loan in the name of the surviving spouse and secure it against the deceased's property while it's held in probate (which may even include real estate). You will need to speak to the bank in relation to any such loan; and preferably a bank with which the deceased or his family have a good relationship as this should make matters easier to facilitate.

Reducing Expenses During those First Few Days

One of the too often overlooked, yet important, tasks that you should attend to in the first few days following a death is the reduction of on-going expenses. This task becomes much more important where the family of the deceased has limited funds available to it until probate of the deceased's estate completes.

It's important to reduce expenses immediately because in death, while revenues generally cease immediately (salary or social security for example), expenses continue to accrue indefinitely. In practice, you will need to sort through, with the assistance of the deceased's family, the personal papers of the deceased in order to see what ongoing expenses he may still have in place.

Here are just a few suggestions as to what can be done: cancel absolutely everything that isn't really required anymore – the deceased's health insurance, phone service, utilities, certain insurances (for example phone insurance, credit card insurance, travel insurance etc), newspaper and magazine subscriptions, club memberships, sports memberships, etc. This list is by no means exhaustive as almost everyone has something they can add to it. This cancellation exercise has a dual benefit – the expenses stops immediately and within a few weeks the estate may well be getting refunds running into thousands of dollars.

Providing for Minor Children

If the deceased left children but no surviving spouse, you will need to consider whether a guardian and/or conservator will need to be appointed if none has been appointed under the terms of the deceased's will. The appointment itself will usually involve a court application and, as such, you should speak to an attorney in order to determine what exactly needs to be done in order to progress the application.

While your role as executor does not involve you directly in the appointment of a guardian for the children, you may be able to help the family consider which of the testator's relatives (or those of a deceased spouse or partner) or friends would be best suited to care for the deceased's children. This is by no means a simple decision and you should afford due thought and consideration before reaching a conclusion. If appropriate and depending on their age, the family may wish to discuss the matter directly with the children in question. Also, review the will to determine if the deceased had appointed any guardians.

 Important Note

Whenever possible, we strongly recommend that an executor discusses all possible guardianship scenarios with the testator before the will is made or as soon as the executor becomes aware of his appointment (assuming of course that this happens before the testator passes away) so that proper provision can be made for the testator's children and so that the executor is aware of all of the options.

Initial Inspection and Protection of Property

While you will not actually be officially appointed as executor until the formal probate process commences, you should (assuming you have not decided to decline the role) still consider taking steps to locate and secure the deceased's assets - be it with insurance cover or otherwise.

There are a number of steps that you can take to locate as many assets as possible. For instance, you can inspect the deceased's bank records and files as well as open any safe deposit boxes held by the deceased. We will discuss the mechanics of this latter point in much more detail below, so for now just bear it in mind as a preliminary task that you may need to tend to.

As an executor, you will also be responsible for the inspection and securing of any real estate in the estate including the continuance or termination of any relevant utilities, as well as, the examination and updating (if necessary) of any fire, casualty and other business insurance. In certain instances, depending on the circumstances, it may even be necessary to consider organizing security systems or personnel to protect the property.

 Important Note

As an executor you will be responsible for the protection of all of the assets of the estate. This includes protection from theft, fire, loss and destruction. If you fail to preserve the assets, you could be held personally liable. A simple way to protect the estate's assets is to take them into your personal possession. This should be done specifically where you acquire valuable documents. Once in your possession, they should be placed in a secured storage facility and, where appropriate, should be insured for full value.

Another important duty of an executor is the assessment of any ongoing small business (previously operated by the testator either alone, in partnership with others or through a corporation or company). You may very well be required to make preliminary management decisions about the running needs of any such business even though the business may operate outside your area of expertise. In such cases, you should consider engaging the services of a professional director, an accountant or other professional who can properly assist with and advise on running the business. In any event, when confronted with the possibility of running a business, it's best to discuss the matter with the deceased's former business partners, any family members or friends that may have been involved in the business with the deceased and/or professional advisors.

Important Note

Where possible, an executor should have a full and detailed discussion with the testator as to how his business would be managed in the short term following his death. This may save the business thousands of dollars and prevent a depletion in the value of the business.

CHAPTER 6:

WHAT AN EXECUTOR SHOULD DO IN THE FIRST MONTH

Chapter Overview

In this chapter, we look at the tasks than an executor must deal with during the first month following his appointment. These tasks include establishing appropriate filing systems, reducing expenses of the estate and managing the assets of the estate. By the end of this chapter, your obligations as executor will become a lot clearer to you!

Chapter

6

CHAPTER 6

WHAT AN EXECUTOR SHOULD DO IN THE FIRST MONTH

Introduction

Following the death of the deceased, your first task will be to ensure that you are ready to carry out your duties as an executor. In preparing yourself, you will need to physically organize yourself for the tasks ahead, gain an understanding of the probate process and locate, collect and manage the estate assets pending their distribution to the beneficiaries named under the deceased's will. We will explore each of these aspects in more detail below.

PART 1 - GETTING ORGANIZED

Set Up a Filing System

Being well organized and maintaining an appropriate filing system is critical to ensuring your success as an executor. You will need to set up a filing system that allows you to keep track of paperwork relating to the deceased's estate – as well as any notes that you make while carrying out probate. Being organized in this manner will help you when it comes to dealing with claims against the estate and dealing with financial institutions and beneficiaries.

Important Note

Be careful not to lose any papers relating to the probate of the deceased's estate or to mix those papers up with your own. This could lead to a situation where you forget about certain assets and close probate of the estate without ever transferring the assets to the rightful beneficiary. If this happens, you may need to re-open probate.

With a little thought, setting up a simple filing system should be a relatively straightforward task. Typically, there are two particular filing systems that you could use. You could either establish a system based on subject category (for example, income, expenses, assets, liabilities, etc) or, alternatively, some form of numerical system. The choice is yours. You can use whatever system makes the most sense to you.

Organizing by Category

The first step in the process will be to sort through your papers and discard anything that you don't need. Alternatively, if you don't wish to discard certain papers, it may be useful to place them in a miscellaneous file. The next step is to sort the papers into various piles or categories. You could consider using some of the following categories:-

- bank statements;

- birth certificates and other personal records;

- brokerage account statements;

- business agreements;

- child support documents;

- credit card statements;

- disability-related documents;

- divorce papers;

- employment related matters;

- insurance policies, statements, or bills;

- investment records;

- pension records;

- post office;

- prenuptial agreement;

- real estate deeds and tax records;

- registration papers for vehicles or boats;

- retirement account statements;

- service providers (e.g., landscapers, trash haulers, etc.);

- social security records;

- state health/welfare departments;

- utility companies; and

- miscellaneous.

Once you have decided on the categories you want to use, create a file or sub file for each category. Clearly label each category. Then sort through the papers that you wish to keep and place them into appropriate categories. If none of the categories seem appropriate, don't be afraid to create a new category – but, remember, don't complicate matters too much.

We recommend placing your files in a suitable filing cabinet or filing system so that the records can be easily accessed and maintained in the future.

Organizing By Number

Similar to the categories system, decide on the papers that you want to keep. Now sort them into bundles. For each bundle, you will create a numerical file. You will then create an index or a spreadsheet identifying that file by reference to its number and detailing the contents of that file. Each new file is given a new number and an appropriate description. When you need to find something, you can simply do a word search of your spreadsheet. If you have properly identified the contents of the file, your search should reveal the number of the file in which the required information is stored.

Of course, the big disadvantage of organizing by numbers or index filing is that you must keep the spreadsheet or document log updated. This can be tedious work, especially if there is a large amount of paperwork associated with the estate.

Filing Tips

Many people often find it easier to organize files by number or alphabetically so that they can be easily found when required. People also like to use similar colored files or similar colored tabs for related sub-categories. This helps to find the file a lot quicker – especially if the files are placed in a well packed cabinet.

Obtain a Tax Identification Number

Before you can deal with the deceased's estate, you will need to obtain an employer's tax identification number or a taxpayer identification number as it is also called. These identification numbers will need to be provided whenever you deal with a financial institution or a third party.

The process of obtaining a new employer identification number is quite straightforward. All you need to do is complete an Internal Revenue Service Form SS-4 and return it to the IRS. Once processed, the IRS should issue you with a tax identification number for the estate. You can obtain the relevant form from the IRS website at http://www.irs.gov/formspubs/index.html or obtain the number online at https://sa2.www4.irs.gov/modiein/individual/index.jsp.

Important Note

All transactions carried out by the estate should be done in the estate's name and using the estate's tax identification number.

Open a Bank Account in the Name of the Estate

The opening of a bank account in the name of the estate goes hand in hand with your obligation to maintain proper financial records for the estate. By using a designated bank account, you will be able to use the account statement to help keep track of all payments made and all benefits received by the estate.

As an executor, you will have the choice of which financial institution you wish to open the account with. In practice, many executors tend to open an account with either the bank with whom they personally deal for their own day to day affairs or with the deceased's bank. Of course, you are more than entitled to evaluate and use other banks especially if it makes financial or commercial sense to do so in the circumstances.

Financial institutions provide varying services that may be required by an executor of an estate. These include services such as the provision of loans, share valuations, trust services, investment management and so on. In deciding on which institution to use, it's important that you properly evaluate the services provided by the institution in question, the likelihood that you will require these services and the likely fees associated with engaging a bank to act in these matters. If chosen correctly, the right financial institution can help you keep legal and other costs down.

Pay attention to the interest rates offered by the various financial institutions – remember the estate's monies may be sitting in the account for a number of months or even years. Where there is a large amount of money sitting in the account, interest payments can be quite significant.

Important Note

Safety checks

When making payments from the estate, it's useful to use 'safety checks'. These are similar to standard checks and can be purchased from most banks. The big difference is that every time you write a check, the details are input on to a carbon copy at the back of the check. You can use this carbon copy to help maintain your records of estate transactions.

Once you have an account set up, you should transfer all the estate's cash and monies to this account and, after that, ensure that all of the estate's transactions are put through that account. It's also important that you only use one account so as to avoid the risk of accidentally mixing up the estate's funds with other monies. Believe it or not this happens quite frequently especially where an executor is the surviving spouse of the deceased. In particular, it's often easy to mix up funds which pass to the estate outside the probate process (such as certain insurance payments or payments under a pay-on-death account) as well as other benefits which are paid directly to the estate. You should ensure that you take appropriate measures to avoid this happening.

PART II

SEARCHING FOR & LOCATING ESTATE ASSETS

Sort Through the Deceased's Personal Belongings

As an executor, you will need to carry out a thorough search for all of the deceased's assets and liabilities. It will be your sole responsibility to locate these assets, to pay any taxes owing on them and, ultimately, to distribute those assets to the beneficiaries named in the deceased's will. Typically, these assets will include items such as real estate, cash, investments, vehicles, social security payments, bank accounts, furniture, antiques, artwork, jewelry, pension plans, IRAs, stocks, brokerage accounts, shares in privately held companies and businesses, partnership interests, life insurance and so on.

Finding assets and determining liabilities is not always an easy task. In some cases the deceased's assets or liabilities may be readily identifiable from the deceased's own personal files or, in the case of certain personal assets, may be conveniently located in the deceased's home. However, in the majority of cases, you will need to carefully review the deceased's personal records and correspondence to establish the assets held or liabilities owing by the deceased at the time of his death.

In carrying out your search, there are a number of places where you can start. In this regard, we recommend that you review the following:-

- any letter of instruction left by the deceased;

- the deceased's check books and banks statements;

- the deceased's mail; and

- any safe deposit box held by the deceased.

Review Letter of Instruction

The task of discovering assets and liabilities would of course be a lot easier if the deceased left an up-to-date letter of instruction listing all of his assets and liabilities, a description of those assets and liabilities and details of the location of the assets and any related title documentation. Of course, even if the deceased left such a list you would still need to make allowances for any assets or liabilities that may have been overlooked when compiling the list. As such, to cover this possibility, you will still need to review the deceased's personal records.

Of course, if there is no letter of instruction and you are not really aware of, or familiar with, the deceased's financial dealings you will just have to carry out your own search the hard way.

Review Check Books and Bank Statements

One of the best and most fruitful places to start your review is with the deceased's financial records. A review of the deceased's check book, cancelled checks, bank statements and credit card statements can reveal a huge amount about the deceased's incomes and expenses. Usually, it's both prudent and useful to review each record or statement on a transaction by transaction basis for the three years prior to the deceased's death.

The records will give you great clues as to the assets and liabilities of the deceased. For instance you will find direct debit details, or check stubs of checks that have been written, for such items as:

- annual subscriptions – magazines, charities, etc;

- charge card accounts;

- dividends;

- insurance policies – travel, medical, vehicle, house, business, etc;

- license fees for cars, boats, guns, business, etc;

- loans – personal, business, etc;

- memberships – gyms, clubs, professional, etc;

- monthly savings, investments, etc;

- mortgage payments;

- payments to brokers;

- rental receipts;

- royalties;

- social security receipts;

- taxes – personal, business, etc;

- rental payments – property, cars, machinery, equipment, etc;

- utility payments – gas, electricity, telephone, cell phone, etc; and

- so on…..

The items listed above are just a sampling of the many items you will come across.

Important Task

Upon discovery, cancel all non-essential ongoing expenditures and seek refunds where appropriate.

In addition to reviewing the deceased's financial records and statements, you should also contact each financial institution at which the deceased held an account to determine the various accounts held by the deceased there and also the balance of those accounts at the date of his death. In most cases, the financial institution will ask for a copy of your letters of authority as well as a certified copy of the death certificate of the deceased before releasing that information to you. Certain institutions may require additional documentation but they will generally advise you where such documents are required.

In certain states, banks and other financial institutions will require the approval of the state taxing authority before it releases the proceeds of an account to the executor of an estate. This approval is not very difficult to obtain, particularly where the beneficiaries of the deceased's estate are close family members of the deceased. The financial institution will advise you if this is required and of the required procedure for obtaining approval.

The Deceased's Mail

Another great source of information regarding the deceased's affairs will come from the deceased's mail. In addition to personal correspondence, the mail will often contain helpful items such as professional correspondence, bank statements, portfolio statements, dividend checks and so on. These documents will all provide useful information regarding the deceased's assets and liabilities.

In order to get the mail, you can of course go to the deceased's home or former place of business and collect it. However, it often makes more sense to re-direct the deceased's mail to your home address or office. In order to re-direct the mail, you will need to contact the U.S. Postal Service directly. In the absence of contacting them, they will continue to deliver the mail to the deceased's residence. A member of the deceased's family can usually change the postal address with a copy of the death certificate and personal identification. However, as an executor you will need to produce evidence of your appointment as executor of the deceased's estate. Usually, the post office will look for a copy of your letters of authority. As you may not yet have your letters of authority (we discuss obtaining your letters of authority in more detail in Chapter 8) you should consult with the deceased's family to make arrangements. You should also contact your local post office in order to get a copy of the form that you will need to complete to register the change of address.

While dealing with the deceased's mail, you might also consider taking the opportunity to have the deceased's name removed from commercial marketing lists. The Direct Marketing Association (**"DMA"**) maintains a Deceased Do Not Contact list. All DMA members are obliged to remove any names appearing on this list from their own mailing lists. Indeed, many non-DMA members review this list and remove the names from their own mailing lists. Once a name is registered with the DMA, both solicited and non-solicited commercial mail should begin to decrease within a few months. To register a name or learn more, you can visit the DMA website at www.the-dma.org.

Safe Deposit Box

If the deceased's records reveal the existence of a safe deposit box, you will want to open it as soon as possible in order to check the contents. Often, safe deposit boxes contain important legal documents such as title deeds, stock certificates, bearer bonds, wills, powers of attorney and so on. In addition, they can often contain jewelry, cash and important physical possessions.

However, before rushing off to open a safe deposit box, it's important that you first understand some of the legalities around how they are 'held' and how they can be opened.

A safe deposit box can be held or registered in the name of one or more people. Where it is held by one person, the holder may designate someone with authority to access it. Where it is held by two people as joint holders, a surviving joint owner will have access to the box after the other joint holder dies. However, if the deceased was the sole registered owner of the box, the bank will typically deny access to the box until an executor or personal representative of the deceased's estate is appointed.

 Did You Know?

There are significant legal consequences associated with the joint holding of a safe deposit box or indeed any other assets. Legal advice may therefore be required when dealing with jointly held safe deposit boxes.

However, on certain occasions, the bank will allow you open the safe deposit box under bank supervision for the purpose of determining whether it contains the deceased's will.

Historically, safe deposit boxes were sealed upon the death of the registered owner in order to secure the payment of state inheritance tax. The boxes could only be opened in the presence of a tax official who would carry out an inventory of its contents upon opening the box. Since state inheritance taxes have been abolished in the majority of states, this limitation should not be a concern in most cases. However, you should check with the bank maintaining the safe deposit box or with an attorney registered in that state as to whether any legalities apply. If there are any formalities, the bank or attorney will advise you on how to proceed.

Whether or not any formalities apply to the opening of a safe deposit box, it's good practice to have a witness attend with you when you are opening a safe deposit box. It's often useful to prepare an inventory in the presence of the witness and have them sign their name at the bottom of the inventory to confirm its accuracy.

PART III

CLAIMING BENEFITS

Claim Unpaid Salary, Insurance and Other Benefits

If the surviving spouse or children of the deceased have not already done so, you should organize for the collection of any salary, wages, accumulated vacation and/or sick pay and other fringe benefits that may be owing to the deceased.

The laws of some states permit the direct payment of salary and other benefits to the surviving spouse, adult children or other next of kin of a deceased employee without the need to have these funds tied up in the probate process. Where state law allows, either you (as executor) or the deceased's family members should have little trouble in collecting these funds from the deceased's employer, although some smaller companies may not be as familiar with the law on this point. In the event of difficulty obtaining payment or undue delay in doing so you should consider engaging an attorney to assist you and, if necessary, file a complaint with the state Department of Labor through a small claims court.

There are numerous different types of benefits that an estate may be entitled to claim including, amongst others:

- life insurance and annuities;

- mortgage insurance;

- survivor's social security benefits;

- employment retirement plan benefits;

- bank account benefits that are payable on death;

- savings bond benefits;

- veteran's benefits;

- social security benefits;

- redeeming traveler's checks; and

- redeeming unused airplane tickets and prepaid travel.

In addition to the above, if there are circumstances which would lead you to the conclusion that the deceased's death occurred as a result of the willful act or negligence of a third party, you should consult an attorney as the estate may be entitled to take a wrongful death action against any person or organization responsible for the deceased's death. The majority of cases for wrongful death are based on claims for medical misdiagnosis, medical negligence, dangerous driving or negligence of some other description.

PART IV

MANAGING THE ESTATE

Managing the Estate

As an executor, it will be your responsibility to ensure that the estate pays any bills that the deceased had outstanding (such as utility or credit card bills) at the time of his death. You can discharge these debts from the existing funds within the estate, from benefits paid to the estate following the deceased's death and from debts owing to the estate at the time of the deceased's death and subsequently recovered.

The management of the estate can be quite straightforward at times. In most cases, executors simply need to manage the estate bank account, pay debts, acknowledge and assess claims against the estate and so on. However, on occasion, matters can become more complex. For example, if the deceased owned a business, you may have to buy or sell certain assets to ensure the survival of the business, make payroll distributions, temporarily run the business (or at the very least, find someone suitably qualified to do it) until it is passed on to the deceased's beneficiaries (of course, the deceased could stipulate in his will that the business be sold or give the executor authority to sell it in order to distribute the estate).

Similar issues could arise where the deceased had large real estate portfolios or complex investment structures. In which case you will most likely need to consult a professional advisor in order to understand how these interests can be passed on to the estate's beneficiaries in a tax efficient manner. Remember, the cost of engaging a professional advisor will be a cost of the estate and not a personal cost of yours – so do not hesitate to engage a professional where you feel it appropriate or necessary.

So, when you are faced with managing the estate, where do you actually start? What do you do first? Well, one of the first things that you need to do is to prevent the depletion of value from the estate. This is done in two ways – firstly, by cutting off any unnecessary expenditures being incurred by the estate and, secondly, by liquidating any assets which are depreciating in value. After that, it's important that the remaining assets are secured and managed until such time as they are ready to be distributed to the beneficiaries under the will. Remember, as an executor, it is your responsibility to ensure that the value of the estate is preserved until that time.

Send Death Notices to the Utilities Companies and Financial Institutions

As soon as possible after the death of the deceased, you should commence the process of canceling all non-essential payments being made by the estate.

In order to do this, you will need to send notifications of cancellation to each relevant party together with a copy of the deceased's death certificate and your letters of authority (if issued).

You will need to contact the various utility companies in order to cancel all non-essential utilities such as gas, electricity, water, telephone, etc. However, you need to be careful in selecting which utilities you wish to cancel. Perhaps the deceased's family will remain in the deceased's house? Maybe the house will be vacant but a harsh winter is expected so it would be prudent to leave the heat on to prevent dampness? Maybe the electricity needs to be kept on in order to operate the security system? Maybe the deceased sub-let his premises to a third party and they need access to the utilities?

The decision to terminate a utility is therefore one which should only be made after due consideration of all related matters.

However, apart from the utilities, there is nothing to prevent you from notifying the banks and credit card companies and requesting that they cease all payments immediately – including both direct debits and standing orders. However, similar to the position above regarding utilities, the payments should only be stopped after a careful review as to why they are being made in the first instance.

As already mentioned, in the case of bank accounts, it's useful to have the funds contained in the deceased's accounts transferred to the estate bank account so that you can easily keep track of payments from one central location. Where you do this, remember to set up appropriate standing orders and direct debits to facilitate payment of any utilities, insurance premiums or other payments that will need to be made.

You will also need to notify the deceased's creditors of the deceased's death so that they can present any claims that they might have against the estate. The payment of creditors is a complicated area and covered in greater detail in Chapter 9.

The deceased's mail is a good source of information to help you determine who or what institutions should be notified of the deceased's death. However, typically, the following institutions need to be notified:-

- banks;

- credit card companies;

- utility companies;

- post office;

- doctors or other health care providers;

- employer and former employers;

- investment firms;

- insurance companies;

- landlord or tenants;

- pension payers;

- service providers (e.g., landscapers, trash haulers, etc.);

- social security administration;

- state health/welfare departments; and

- veteran affairs department.

You should also notify the Social Security Administration (www.ssa.gov) of the deceased's death. If the deceased was receiving Social Security payments, they may require you to return or refund any check received by the deceased in the month in which he died.

Finally, if the deceased was in receipt of spousal or child support from a spouse or former spouse, you should advise the spouse or former spouse of the deceased's death.

Cancel Unnecessary Estate Expenses

It's important to cancel all unnecessary expenses of the estate and not just utility bills. In this respect, you should:-

- terminate any rental arrangements which the deceased had whereby he/she rented or leased property as a tenant/lessee (be it for personal or commercial purposes) at the time of his death. Remember, in addition to real estate, such arrangement may include lease purchase equipment arrangements, vehicle leasing arrangements and much more. Alternatively, if it is not possible to terminate the arrangement, consider sub-letting or sub-leasing the property/equipment to a third party. The ability of the deceased's estate to terminate or sublease the property will be determined by the terms of the property/equipment lease. In certain cases, the lease may automatically expire on the death of the deceased. As such, it would be a useful exercise for you to review the terms of the lease or, alternatively, engage a real estate attorney to do so on your behalf. The ultimate goal here is to reduce costs;

- terminate any lease purchase arrangements (if possible);

- cancel driver's license, magazine, newspaper and newsletter subscriptions (remember some of these may be internet based – so check the deceased's credit card for clues), cable and satellite television, gym and club memberships and so on. In some cases, where these services or memberships are cancelled before expiry and have already been paid for in full it is possible to obtain refunds. Contact the relevant organization to see what their refund policy is;

- cancel all annual subscriptions and professional memberships;

- cancel health insurance, medical insurance and travel insurance coverage;

- consider whether it would be appropriate to cancel auto insurance, boat insurance, house insurance, pet insurance and any other insurance;

- cancel all credit cards and seek refunds on any gift cards;

- complete or cancel outstanding broker's orders; and

- cancel standing orders and direct debits.

Dealing With Depreciating Assets

As executor, you will be responsible for preserving the value of the deceased's estate. Hand in hand with that responsibility is the obligation to dispose of any assets that are depreciating in value. By converting these 'wasting assets' into cash, it will be a lot easier to preserve the overall value of the estate.

Depreciation generally occurs where an item suffers loss in value usually due to wear, use or age. We typically think of cars as depreciating assets. The older a car gets and the more miles it has driven the less valuable it becomes. Houses, on the other hand, tend to appreciate in value. Of course, this is not always the case. For example, where a house is left vacant for a prolonged period of time it will begin to deteriorate as no one is maintaining it on a regular basis. Where this occurs, the costs of maintaining the house can rise substantially and the house itself can become more vulnerable to vandalism. In such instances, the maintenance of the house can become quite costly for the estate over time. As such, a timely sale of the property will often place the estate in a better financial position overall.

As an executor, it will be your responsibility to identify so called 'wasting assets' – assets which are depreciating or which cost too much too maintain having regard to their value. Once identified, you should consider selling the asset.

In that way, you can preserve the value of the asset in cash and eliminate the incidental costs associated with the maintenance of the asset.

However, before you go to sell the asset, you will need to review the terms of the will to ensure that you have sufficient power to dispose of the asset. Generally speaking, where you have sufficient power and the assets have not been specifically bequeathed to someone under the terms of the deceased's will, you will be free to dispose of the asset without the court's consent. However, if the assets have been left to a specific individual, you should obtain the consent of the court before selling the asset or the written consent of all beneficiaries under the will. Similarly, if you lack sufficient power under the deceased's will to sell the assets, you will also need to obtain the consent of the court before you can sell the asset.

 Important Tip

Don't forget – you cannot sell or deal with the estate assets until such time as you have been formally appointed as an executor of the estate!

Securing Assets

In the majority of cases, the deceased's assets are relatively simple to identify and therefore relatively easy to secure. They usually consist of such items as furnishings, clothing, jewelry, money, securities, residential and investment properties, motor vehicles and the likes. As soon as you have been issued your letters of authority appointing you as executor you can commence the task of securing these assets. In the meantime, you can advise the deceased's family to do so.

Securing the assets of the estate typically includes the following acts:-

- redirecting the deceased's mail to your address;

- arranging for the safe storage of personal valuables, assets and important legal documents. Depending on the assets in question, you may wish to consider placing the assets in a safe deposit box, bank vault or legal document vault;

- reviewing property and vehicle insurance arrangements, maintaining appropriate cover and arranging for any new or additional cover which you deem appropriate;

- if the deceased's home, office or business premises is vacant following the deceased's death, advising the insurance company of this and arranging to have someone check the property or properties regularly;

- cancelation of any unnecessary expenses (see above);

- advising financial institutions, utilities, government bodies and associations of the deceased's death as required;

- if the deceased received benefits under a private insurance policy, contact the insurer to advise of the deceased's death and arrange payment of any sums owing under the policy. Arrange for the collection of all other benefits due to the deceased;

- if the deceased was an executor of another's estate whose administration was not complete at the time of the deceased's death, or was a trustee of a trust, you should advise the other executors or trustees (if any) of the deceased's death and, especially where there are no joint office holders, obtain professional advice as to whether you have any continuing responsibilities arising from your position as executor in respect of the other administration or trust. It's important that you take legal advice in such instances; and

- if the deceased carried on business as a sole proprietor or as the owner-manager of a corporation, then you will need to make arrangements for the continued management of the business and/or for the security of all physical assets and documents of the business. You should consider engaging professional advisors or experienced managers where you decide to carry on the business. Remember, as an executor you are required to act prudently in the management of the estate's assets. Therefore, where it is prudent to take professional advice or engage experienced personnel you should do so.

Managing Personal Property

You will need to visit the deceased's home and make an inventory list of all the deceased's tangible household personal property which will go through the probate process. If you are in any doubt as to whether particular assets will need to go through probate, contact an attorney. The inventory must include a fair market value of each asset as well as details of any outstanding loans or liens against those assets. In order to determine the value of each of the assets in question, you can use the value that the asset would be expected to achieve at an auction of the estate assets. If no auction is planned, then your honest and reasonable "best-guess" estimate of value will usually be acceptable.

The level of detail required for an inventory can vary from case to case. In the ordinary course, it's acceptable to group all of the assets into broad categories such as clothes, furniture, personal effects and the likes. However, bigger items such as vehicles and valuable antiques or jewelry should be listed separately. When valuing these 'big ticket' items, you should use an appropriate valuation method – such as a reliable trade magazine or appraiser.

As the cost of maintaining assets can sometimes exceed the value of the assets themselves, you will need to decide what to do with them once you have listed and valued them.

Where the estate is clearly in a position to discharge all creditor claims against the deceased's estate as well as all expenses and taxes of the estate, you should consider making an application to court to make an early distribution of some of the assets to the beneficiaries. In this way, you will shift the burden of maintaining and insuring the assets to the beneficiary and away from the estate – thereby preventing the further depletion of the estate's assets. Alternatively, you could petition the court to grant you permission to sell the assets in question – this will be required where you have no power of sale under the terms of the will. Again, as mentioned above, if the asset in question has been bequeathed to someone, you should obtain the consent of the beneficiaries before making the sale.

Managing Real Estate

Before we look at the management of real estate, it's important that you understand the different ways in which real estate can be legally held by the deceased. This will help you understand whether the real estate needs to be probated and also what you can and cannot do with it.

Whether or not real estate owned by the deceased at the time of his death will need to go through probate will depend on how the title to that property was held at the time of his death. Typically, property can be held in one of four different ways:-

- joint tenancy with a right of survivorship;

- tenancy by the entireties;

- tenancy in common; and

- community property.

Joint Tenancy With a Right of Survivorship

Where a property is held under a joint tenancy, each of the property owners has an undivided percentage interest in the entire property. To illustrate this, an example is often useful. So let's, for example, take a case where four people own a property equally under a joint tenancy arrangement. Each of the four owners has an entitlement to a 25% interest in the entire or whole of the property. However, because each owner has a right to a percentage of the whole, rather than having a divided and defined 25% interest in the property, he is entitled to access and take actions in respect of the entire property and not simply 25% of it.

Where a joint tenant dies, his share passes to the remaining joint tenants. Taking our example again, where one of the four property owners die, his share passes to each of the other three survivors automatically and each of the survivors then becomes entitled to a 33.33% interest in the property. This is an example of the principle of survivorship in operation.

The key point to take from the example above is that the share passes from the deceased joint owner to the remaining joint owners by operation of law without the need for probate.

Tenancy By the Entireties

A special type of joint tenancy known as a 'tenancy by the entirety' is recognized between married couples in certain states. Under this form of joint ownership, if a married couple owns property as tenants in the entirety, then each spouse must obtain the consent of the other before dealing with the property in any way that would affect the rights of the other. This even includes putting in place a mortgage over the property. Each spouse lacks the power to freely dispose of their interest under their will, or in any other way, as the principle of survivorship applies between the spouses.

 Did You Know?

States that recognize a 'tenancy by the entirety' include: Alaska*, Arkansas, Delaware, District of Columbia, Florida, Hawaii, Illinois*, Indiana*, Kentucky*, Maryland, Massachusetts, Michigan*, Mississippi, Missouri, New Jersey, New York*, North Carolina*, Ohio, Oklahoma, Oregon, Pennsylvania, Rhode Island, Tennessee, Utah, Vermont, Virginia and Wyoming.

* States that allow tenancy by entirety for real estate only.

Tenancy in Common

A tenancy in common is one of the most common forms of property ownership in most states. A tenancy in common is created where two or more people purchase a property together as 'tenants in common'. As tenants in common, each of the parties own a separate and distinguishable part of the property. To take the example of our four property owners above, if the arrangement was a tenancy in common, each of them would own 25% of the property in their own right and would be free to sell that 25% to any person at any time and/or to dispose of their interest under their will. The right of survivorship does not apply here.

Community Property

Community property states have different rules governing probate, so it's important to understand these rules.

At the date of writing there are nine community property states namely Arizona, California, Idaho, Louisiana, Nevada, New Mexico, Texas, Washington and Wisconsin. In Alaska, couples can opt to have their property treated as community property under the terms of a written property agreement. Each of these states has special laws that dictate how married people can own and dispose property – both real and personal.

Did You Know?

Real property is property such as land, buildings and real estate generally. Personal property can be broadly defined as including all other property which a person can own.

In a community property state, the law broadly provides that all earnings generated during the course of a marriage and all property purchased during the marriage is considered community property and therefore equally owned by each spouse. Therefore if, for example, one spouse earns $100,000 per year as an executive, while the other earns $40,000 as a freelance writer, then each spouse shall be deemed to "own" $70,000 of those earnings. In addition to salary, property purchased by one spouse in his own name with money he earned during the marriage will also be regarded as community property. Similarly, debts incurred by either spouse during their marriage are regarded as debts of the couple rather than that of the individual who incurred it.

Separate property, on the other hand, includes property received by a spouse during their marriage by means of a gift or bequest under a will. It also includes any property owned by a spouse before they got married which that spouse has kept segregated from community property during the marriage. Similar to the position regarding debts above, all debts incurred by spouses prior to marriage are considered separate debts of each spouse.

Separate property can also include anything that one spouse gives up in favor of the other spouse in writing.

The distinction between community property and separate property becomes important when determining which of a spouse's assets can be freely disposed of under the terms of their will. In community property states, on the death of a spouse, half of the community property owned by the couple will go to the surviving spouse, unless the deceased spouse's will directs otherwise (i.e. provides for the transfer of part or all of their share of the community property to the surviving spouse). Otherwise, the surviving spouse is free to dispose of their share of community property as well as their separate property as they desire.

Management of Property

Now that you understand the different methods in which real estate can be held, we can look at the management of the real estate. Remember, you do not need to maintain or manage property which passes to another person as a matter of law, under a joint tenancy or tenancy by the entireties arrangement, at the time of the deceased's death.

As an executor, you are therefore required to maintain all other real estate owned by the deceased at the time of his death. This real estate includes the deceased's home, investment properties and land. The funds necessary to maintain the real estate can be taken from the estate's funds. In addition to discharging maintenance costs, you will also need to discharge any mortgage payments, taxes, rates and insurance premiums owing in respect of the properties in order to ensure that the properties are not placed at risk – whether from foreclosure, excessive tax penalties or otherwise.

Managing Cash Accounts and Investments

The management of cash accounts is perhaps one of the easiest tasks you will have as an executor. You simply need to arrange to have the proceeds of the cash account transferred to the estate bank account. In that way you will be better able to manage the proceeds and to use them to discharge debts as the need arises.

On the other hand, all non-liquid assets, such as investments, require appraisal – with the value of most securities being able to be determined easily by consulting either the Wall Street Journal or other listings and bond tables as of the date of the deceased's death. Once you have determined the value of the securities, you will need to decide whether it is prudent to hold on to the securities or liquidate them. Where the securities have been left to a beneficiary under the terms of the will, you should get the consent of the beneficiary before you dispose of them.

The difficulty with holding on to the securities is that their value rises and falls quite frequently. As you are obliged to take prudent steps to maintain the value of the estate's assets you may feel inclined to sell the securities as soon as possible – if the terms of the will permit. Alternatively, you may seek the court's approval to make an early distribution of the securities to the beneficiaries where there is a surplus of assets in the estate. You could even decide to hold the securities until probate has been complete in its entirety in the hope that the value of the securities might rise. In which case the securities could then be sold and applied towards the payment of debts or the proceeds distributed to the beneficiaries. However, before you decide to retain the securities, you should take proper professional advice as to the likelihood of the securities rising or falling in value – otherwise you could be held liable for a beach of your duty to act prudently and in the best interest of the estate.

Under the terms of a will, many executors are empowered to invest the estate funds in securities and other asset classes. However, given the nature of securities, you should be very careful as to how you invest the funds and at the very least should obtain professional advice in advance. In doing so, be mindful of the broker fees and commissions which apply.

As an alternative to investing in securities, you could always consider investing in federally insured interest bearing accounts or in government bonds. In each case, the level of risk is quite low due to the fact that the government has underwritten the investments. Similar to government securities, many financial institutions offer short-term capital secure investments which you ought to consider. Remember, you must act prudently in the selection of the estate's investments – the money is not yours to risk.

Managing a Business

The management of a business can be one of the most difficult tasks you face during the course of probating an estate. With the increased complexity associated with the management of a business comes increased responsibility to ensure that the business is properly managed. The complexity is often such that prudence would require that you engage an expert to help assess the value of the business and to assist with the operation of the business pending its sale or distribution to the beneficiaries. Like the majority of executors, you may not have a vast degree of experience or indeed interest in running a business. As such, you may want to sell the business or turn it over to the beneficiaries under the will as soon as possible. However, if the deceased was not directly involved in the management of the business or if the business employs personnel who are capable of running the business, you may be content to allow it continue in operation for the time being.

The decision as to what happens with the business will of course be determined under the provisions of the deceased's will and/or in accordance with the provisions of any agreement governing the ownership of the business such as a partnership agreement or shareholders' agreement. As an executor you should review all documents carefully to see how the ownership of the business is to be dealt with following the deceased's death. Many of these agreements provide for the valuation of the deceased's share of the business on his death and the subsequent transfer of his interest to the remaining owners of the business.

Where the will provides for the carrying on of the business, you will be permitted to do so pending transfer to the beneficiaries. On the other hand, if no provision is made, you will need to make arrangements to have the business sold or wound up. Generally, state law will stipulate a period in which the business must be wound up. Where you exceed that period, you may need to petition the court to allow extra time to facilitate the winding up.

 Important Note

If you decide to carry on the business for a period of time, we recommend that you consult a lawyer to ensure that you are fully apprised of the tax, commercial and employment law issues associated with the continuance of the business.

Sole Proprietorships

In the absence of the deceased's will providing guidance as to what should happen to a sole proprietorship owned by the deceased, you will need to determine whether it is in the best interests of the estate to close the business immediately or, with the consent of the beneficiaries, keep it in operation until it can be transferred to them. You will need to speak to the beneficiaries to determine whether they would prefer to sell or liquidate the business or maintain it as a 'going concern'.

Of course, if the estate does not have sufficient resources to meet its tax obligations or to discharge taxes, you may need to sell some or all of the business in any event. Again, consult the beneficiaries if you plan to do this as it may be possible to save the business by securing a loan for the purposes of paying the outstanding debts and taxes. Where a decision is made to liquidate or sell the business, you should still consider engaging a suitably qualified and experienced professional to manage the business in the short term. Remember, you are still under a duty to preserve the value of the business.

The preservation of the value of the business will be important from the point of view of ensuring that the estate gets the best possible value for the business. In fact, in selling the business, as executor, you will be under a duty to obtain the best possible value for the business and in due course you may need to justify this value to the beneficiaries. It is therefore prudent to engage the services of an accountant or valuation expert to assist with the determination of the value of the business.

As mentioned above, you will need to carefully consider whether to maintain and manage a business pending its transfer to the beneficiaries under the will. A decision to maintain the business will normally be made in the following circumstances:

- where the will provides for the retention of the business interest without any liability to the executor (other than for fraud, willful misconduct or negligence);

- the requirement to manage the business will be for a short time only and the beneficiaries have indicated that they want to retain the business; and

- the business is making a profit and its retention does not pose an unreasonable risk to the estate.

Notwithstanding that there is in fact good reason to retain the business, certain matters need to be considered before a final decision is made. These include consideration of the following issues:

- does the executor have a good understanding of how the business operates?

- are the current management team and employees capable of carrying on the business profitably?

- is the management team trustworthy? Would it be prudent to appoint an independent person to the management team?

- are there sufficient reporting and accounting systems in place to allow the executor and the estate accountant to monitor the performance of the business?

- will the business be able to meet its obligations as they fall due?

- do the future projections for the business make it a worthwhile long term investment or would it be best to sell up now?

- are there any current or potential business liability issues? If so, are they manageable?

Partnerships

Ordinarily, under partnership law, the death of a partner dissolves the partnership, unless there is an agreement between the partners which provides to the contrary. In practice, most business partnerships have agreements in place which regulate the transfer of partnership interests following the death of one of the partners. In most cases, in order to protect the partnership from the introduction of unwanted third parties, the partnership agreement allows the remaining partners to buy out the deceased partner's interest at a price to be determined in accordance with a valuation mechanism set out in the partnership agreement.

Where the partnership is dissolved, the surviving partners are responsible for winding up the partnership affairs and will be required to present an accounting to you as executor of the deceased partner's estate. If there is a profit on dissolution, the estate will receive its share. However, the opposite is also true. If the partnership makes a loss, the estate may need to contribute to the payment of the deceased's share of any outstanding debts.

Limited Liability Companies

Generally, where a shareholder of a limited liability company or a privately owned corporation dies, his shares will form part of his estate and he will be able to leave them as he pleases to his beneficiaries under the terms of his will or trust, as the case may be. This general rule is however subject to a number of exceptions.

It is common for shareholders in a company to enter into a shareholders' agreement in order to regulate their relationship as owners of that company. Shareholder agreements typically include provisions which entitle the remaining shareholders to acquire the shares of a deceased shareholder following the death of that shareholder. In addition, these rights of acquisition or rights of first refusal are often incorporated in to the by-laws or constitutional documents of the company. The acquisition provisions typically provide a mechanism for valuing the shareholding held by the deceased shareholder and entitle the remaining shareholders to acquire the shares from the executor or the beneficiaries at that valuation.

Where the surviving shareholders exercise their rights to acquire the deceased's shares in the company, you will only really need to concern yourself with receiving the money rather than focusing on the management of the business. Remember to verify that the surviving shareholders do have this right to buy the deceased's shares and get legal advice if you need to.

Until the ownership of the shares is formally transferred to the beneficiary of the deceased's estate (rather than to any of the existing shareholders), you will need to exercise the voting rights attaching to those shares. To exercise these rights to vote, you will need to formally re-register these shares in your name (as executor of the deceased's estate). The company secretary of the company can advise you as to the precise requirements in this respect.

Also, even if the shares are to pass to the beneficiaries under the terms of the deceased's will, you will also need to consider whether to manage the deceased's interest in the business pending that transfer. In formulating your decision, the same considerations as outlined above in relation to 'sole proprietorships' will apply.

Remember if you are in any doubt as to your rights under the terms of a shareholders' agreement or under the by-laws of a company, consult an attorney experienced in this area.

Managing Debts of the Estate

As an executor, it will be your responsibility to ensure that the estate discharges all of the deceased's debts, including unpaid bills, medical expenses, funeral costs, loans and income taxes.

Having reviewed the deceased's personal belongings and mail and having contacted various financial institutions you should have a very good idea of the debts owing by the estate. Where there is a surplus of assets you should consider which debts should be paid immediately (such as mortgage and insurance payments) and which should be left on the back burner until the estate has been finalized. In the normal course, you should only arrange to make payments on behalf of the estate following your appointment as executor.

However, circumstances will invariably arise where certain payments will need to be made before your appointment in order to preserve the estate. For example, a mortgage payment may need to be made to prevent foreclosure. In such cases, you should use good judgment to determine what ought to be paid in advance of your appointment and, where possible, obtain the written consent of the beneficiaries.

Remember, that you should only pay debts which are validly owed by the estate and which are enforceable against the estate. If you are in any doubt as to what is or is not validly owed, you should contact an attorney.

Before you discharge any debts, you will need to determine the precise level of debts owed by the deceased so as to ensure that the estate has sufficient money to pay them all. If there are insufficient funds to discharge the debts in full, after the sale of the estate assets, then you will need to pay certain debts in priority to others. In certain cases, depending on the size of the estate, you can ignore the debts completely. We will discuss the rules of priority and payment of debts in greater detail in Chapter 9. However, for the moment, it's important that you are simply aware of these matters.

Dealing With Taxes

We will discuss the precise taxes payable by the estate in more detail in Chapter 10. Having read that chapter, you can correspond with the local tax office with a view to making the necessary tax returns. You will find the IRS website quite helpful when it comes to explaining the precise returns that need to be made.

Of course, if tax computations are not your forte, you can engage a tax attorney or an accountant to assist with calculating any estate taxes or income taxes which are due by the estate.

More on taxes in Chapter 10.

Keep Copies of All Documents

Finally and while it might go without saying, be sure to keep copies of all records relating to the estate for at least two years following its closure. Also, keep receipts for all expenses you incurred. Remember also that as an executor you are entitled to be reimbursed from the proceeds of the estate for personal expenses incurred in settling the estate!

EXECUTOR CHECKLIST

To get a better understanding of what has to be done during probate administration, here is a checklist of duties you can use.

Duty	Due Date	Completed
File the deceased's will with court		
Inventory the deceased assets		
Open probate of the estate		
Give notice of your appointment to the heirs and beneficiaries		
Verify insurance coverage where needed		
Compute approximate taxes and administrative expenses		
Secure assets		
Identify creditors and pay debts		
Send notice to creditors		
Publish a notice to creditors in newspaper		

Duty	Due Date	Completed
File proof of mailing and publication		
Apply for tax identification number		
Open estate bank account		
Transfer funds to estate account		
Collect life insurance		
File/mail inventory		
File the deceased's final income tax return		
Decide on estate's fiscal year		
File income tax returns for the estate		
File federal estate tax return and pay any taxes due		
File state estate tax return and pay any taxes due		
Make distributions		
Pay administrative expenses		
Prepare final report or account		
Pay expenses of administration		
Final report or account		
File receipts for distribution		
Close estate		

Duty	Due Date	Completed
Seek an order of discharge		

You'll learn more about the matters appearing in this list in the ensuing chapters.

CHAPTER 7:

PROPERTY THAT DOESN'T GO THROUGH PROBATE

Chapter Overview

Not all property passes through probate. In this chapter, we look at the various types of property that can be passed directly to beneficiaries without the need for probate.

CHAPTER 7

PROPERTY THAT DOESN'T GO THROUGH PROBATE

When is Probate Necessary?

As already discussed, probate is a court supervised administrative process by which the assets of a deceased person are gathered - applied to pay debts, taxes and probate expenses - and then distributed to the beneficiaries named in the deceased's last will and testament.

While some states have procedures to allow for a speedy probate process for 'small estates', the average probate takes more than six months to complete. Of course, if there are any difficulties in locating beneficiaries or assets, or if there is any legal challenge in relation to the validity of the deceased's will, this time frame can be increased dramatically and probate can end up taking several years to complete. Any resulting delay could have an adverse effect on the deceased's beneficiaries who may have to wait until the probate is completed before receiving their inheritances.

Probate can also be quite expensive – particularly where it drags on for months on end. In fact, when all the related costs are added up, probate can often cost between 1% and 7% (or even more) of the value of the deceased's probatable estate - and that's just for a normal probate not one that is complex or delayed! Given that probate costs are set by state law, there is very little that anyone can do to mitigate or reduce them - other than utilize one or more of the known probate avoidance measures discussed in this chapter.

The legal mechanisms most commonly used to avoid probate include:-

- payable on death, transfer on death or joint accounts;

- insurance policies;

- joint ownership of property;

- revocable living trusts;

- lifetime gifts; and

- others.

These particular methods have a number of advantages. For example, they are flexible and easy to set up. Bank accounts and insurance policies can be established, amended and terminated with little hassle or cost. As a result, the account holder can quickly and easily change the beneficiaries of his assets or the amount by which he intends them to benefit by means of a simple visit to his local bank or insurance broker. And after he passes away, the only document that his beneficiaries should need to present to the bank or insurance company in order to receive the proceeds of their inheritance is a death certificate evidencing his death. With that, the financial institution should be willing to make arrangements to have the relevant proceeds transferred to the beneficiary's name or paid out to him or her.

However, there are also disadvantages to using these methods. In particular, the account holder needs to be very careful to ensure that all of his probate alternatives are working together to avoid probate and, more importantly, to distribute his assets in accordance with the overall objectives of his estate plan. He will need to pay close attention to the beneficiaries named in joint bank accounts and insurance policies, the manner in which real estate is held, the terms of his will, and so on. Any lack of attention could result in one person receiving a lot more than was intended - to the detriment of someone else. Of course, by the time the problem materializes the account holder may not be around to remedy it.

We discuss each of the above probate avoidance mechanisms in more detail in the ensuing pages.

Payable on Death or Transfer on Death Accounts

One of easiest ways to avoid probate is by having a pay on death ("**POD**") or transfer on death ("**TOD**") account. The majority of states now have laws that allow account holders to designate a named beneficiary who will receive the proceeds of his bank and/or investment accounts after they have died. When the account holder dies, the money in the designated account goes directly to the named beneficiary without going through probate.

Important Note

In certain states, POD accounts are referred to as Totten Trusts after the famous New York case (In re Totten) which related to pay on death accounts.

As an executor, you should check to see if any of the deceased's accounts contain a 'POD designation'. The relevant financial institution will be able to give you information in this respect. TOD accounts are similar to POD accounts but are more commonly used to transfer ownership of stocks, bonds and mutual funds.

Transfer on Death Securities

The Transfer on Death Security Registration Act provides for the transfer on death of stocks, shares, bonds and other financial instruments and securities. Similar to the TOD and POD accounts referred to above, these securities can be transferred on death to named beneficiaries free of the requirement to pass through probate.

To date, the following states have adopted the legislation:-

STATE	STATUS	EFFECTIVE DATE	STATE	STATUS	EFFECTIVE DATE
Alabama	*PASSED*	May 29, 1997	Montana	*PASSED*	Oct 1, 1993
Alaska	*PASSED*	Jan 1, 1997	Nebraska	*PASSED*	Sep 9, 1993
Arizona	*PASSED*	Jan 1, 1996	Nevada	*PASSED*	Jun 1, 1997
Arkansas	*PASSED*	Aug 13, 1993	New Hampshire	*PASSED*	Jun 18, 1997
California	*PASSED*	Jan 1, 1999	New Jersey	*PASSED*	Sep 20, 1995
Colorado	*PASSED*	Jul 1, 1990	New Mexico	*PASSED*	Jul 1, 1992
Connecticut	*PASSED*	May 14, 1997	New York	*PASSED*	Jan 1, 2006
Delaware	*PASSED*	Jun 26, 1996	North Carolina	*PASSED*	Oct 1, 2005
District of Columbia	*PASSED*	Apr 27, 2001	North Dakota	*PASSED*	Jul 1, 1991
Florida	*PASSED*	Jan 1, 1995	Ohio	*PASSED*	Oct 1, 1993
Georgia	*PASSED*	Jul 1, 1999	Oklahoma	*PASSED*	Sep 1, 1994
Hawaii	*PASSED*	Apr 29, 1998	Oregon	*PASSED*	Sep 29, 1991
Idaho	*PASSED*	Jul 1, 1996	Pennsylvania	*PASSED*	Dec 18, 1996
Illinois	*PASSED*	Jan 1, 1995	Rhode Island	*PASSED*	Jul 9, 1998
Indiana	*PASSED*	Jul 1, 1997	South Carolina	*PASSED*	Jun 13, 1997

STATE	STATUS	EFFECTIVE DATE	STATE	STATUS	EFFECTIVE DATE
Iowa	*PASSED*	May 26, 1997	South Dakota	*PASSED*	Jul 1, 1996
Kansas	*PASSED*	Jul 1, 1994	Tennessee	*PASSED*	Jul 1, 1995
Kentucky	*PASSED*	Aug 1, 1998	Texas	-	-
Louisiana	-	-	Utah	*PASSED*	May 1, 1995
Maine	*PASSED*	Mar 27, 1998	Vermont	*PASSED*	Jul 1, 1999
Maryland	*PASSED*	Oct 1, 1994	Virginia	*PASSED*	Jul 1, 1994
Massachusetts	*PASSED*	Nov 5, 1998	Washington	*PASSED*	Jul 25, 1993
Michigan	*PASSED*	Dec 20, 1996	West Virginia	*PASSED*	Jun 8, 1994
Minnesota	*PASSED*	Jun 1, 1992	Wisconsin	*PASSED*	May 11, 1990
Mississippi	*PASSED*	Mar 24, 1997	Wyoming	*PASSED*	Jul 1, 1993
Missouri	*PASSED*	Jan 1, 1990			

Retirement Accounts

Similar to POD accounts, it's also possible to designate beneficiaries of retirement accounts such as IRAs and 401(k)s. On the deceased's death, the designated beneficiaries will become entitled to the proceeds of those accounts free from the need to have those proceeds go through the probate process. It is important that the beneficiary must be designated on the account documents and NOT in the deceased's last will, living trust or elsewhere. If the deceased has not designated the beneficiary on the account documents, the proceeds will end up going through probate and there will be no guarantee that the funds will be available to the named beneficiary after that process has completed.

Joint Accounts

Another easy way to avoid probate is by using joint accounts. Where an account is held in the name of two or more persons and is designated with the right of survivorship, then when one of the account holders die, the surviving account holders will automatically acquire the deceased account holder's interest in the account. Whoever is the last surviving joint owner will ultimately own the proceeds of the account outright.

Where a transfer occurs on survivorship, there is no need for probate. The surviving account holder(s) will simply need to provide a copy of the deceased account holder's death certificate to the bank and the bank can then remove that person's name from the account.

The relevant financial institution should be able to advise whether the account was held with a right of survivorship designation.

Custodial Accounts

People often decide to set aside funds in the form of bank accounts, certificates of deposit or similar securities as a nest egg for their minor children, grandchildren or others, to cover things like college expenses or simply to give them a start in life. One of the most common ways of doing this is by means of a custodial account.

When a custodial account is set up, a beneficiary will be named as the person entitled to receive the proceeds of that account upon reaching a designated age. Until the beneficiary reaches that age, a person known as a custodian will manage the cash and assets (such as stocks) in that account on behalf of the beneficiary. Once the person who established the account transfers cash or assets to the account, the title and ownership of those assets immediately vests in the beneficiary. This of course means that the person who transferred the assets to the account can't simply ask for them back.

If the account generates any income, that too will be deemed to be the property of the beneficiary and tax returns may need to be made as a result.

The account will automatically terminate when the beneficiary reaches a specified or designated age. The relevant age of termination is set out under the Uniform Gifts to Minors Act, 1956 and the Uniform Transfers to Minors Act, 1986. In some cases, the exact age of termination is specified while in others the person who created the custodial account will have the ability to choose between a small range of ages such as between 18 to 21.

AGE LIMITS FOR PROPERTY MANAGEMENT IN UTMA STATES			
State	Age at Which Minor Gets Property	State	Age at Which Minor Gets Property
Alabama	21	Missouri	21
Alaska	18 to 25	Montana	21
Arizona	21	Nebraska	21
Arkansas	18 to 21	Nevada	18 to 25
California	18 to 25	New Hampshire	21
Colorado	21	New Jersey	18 to 21
Connecticut	21	New Mexico	21
Delaware	21	New York	21
District of Columbia	18 to 21	North Carolina	18 to 21
Florida	21	North Dakota	21
Georgia	21	Ohio	18 to 21
Hawaii	21	Oklahoma	18 to 21

AGE LIMITS FOR PROPERTY MANAGEMENT IN UTMA STATES			
State	Age at Which Minor Gets Property	State	Age at Which Minor Gets Property
Idaho	21	Oregon	21 to 25
Illinois	21	Pennsylvania	21 to 25
Indiana	21	Rhode Island	21
Iowa	21	South Dakota	18
Kansas	21	Tennessee	21 to 25
Kentucky	18	Texas	21
Maine	18 to 21	Utah	21
Maryland	21	Virginia	18 to 21
Massachusetts	21	Washington	21
Michigan	18 to 21	West Virginia	21
Minnesota	21	Wisconsin	21
Mississippi	21	Wyoming	21

From a probate perspective, custodial accounts are important because the assets in the account will not be deemed to be the property of the account creator at the time of his death for the purposes of probate - as title to the proceeds in that account passed to the named beneficiary upon transfer to the account.

Savings Bonds

Saving bonds can be held jointly between one or more people and, like POD accounts, can contain a pay on death designation. Where such a designation is added, the bonds will pass into the name of the surviving bond holder(s) upon the death of one of the other bondholders. This will happen without the need to have the bonds cashed or for them to go through the probate process.

If the bonds are not held jointly or if there is no POD designation, the bonds can only be redeemed by the executor of the deceased's estate. As such, they will form part of the deceased's probatable estate. However, the bonds may be reissued to a beneficiary under a will upon a request from the executor accompanied by a copy of the death certificate and the executor's letters of authority. As such, assuming that the estate is able to meet all its debt and tax obligations, you could request that the bonds be re-issued in the name of the beneficiary named under the will – if there is one of course. If the value of those bonds has grown since the date of death of the bondholder, income tax may be due as a result of the death of the bondholder. Also, this would be deemed to be an early distribution of estate assets, so the previously outlined considerations would apply.

Life Insurance Proceeds

A life policy is another example of a simple means by which probate can be avoided. Where the deceased designated a named beneficiary under his life insurance policy, the proceeds of that policy will be paid directly to the named beneficiary on his death without the need to go through probate. However, if the deceased's estate is named as the beneficiary of the policy, or if no beneficiaries have been named, or if the named beneficiaries have died, the proceeds will become part of the deceased's estate and will need to pass through the probate process before they can be distributed to the beneficiaries named in the deceased's will. If no beneficiaries have been named in the deceased's will, the proceeds will pass to the residuary beneficiaries.

Even where insurance proceeds are paid directly to a designated beneficiary on the deceased's death, they will still be considered to be part of the deceased's estate for federal estate tax purposes and, in the normal course, will be taxable.

Joint Ownership of Property

As mentioned in Chapter 6, whether or not the property that you own at the time of your death will need to be probated depends on how the title to that property is held. If property was held jointly with a right of survivorship then it will pass to the surviving joint owner(s) automatically by operation of law on the death of the joint owner, without the need to go through probate.

For more information on the joint ownership of property, see Chapter 6.

Revocable Living Trust

An additional way to avoid probate is to establish and fund a revocable living trust. This type of trust is established by means of a written trust agreement or deed made between the creator of the trust, acting as 'grantor,' and the creator of the trust acting as 'trustee'.

Under the terms of the trust agreement, the grantor will transfer ownership of certain of his assets into the name of the trust. Once in the trust, these assets will be managed by the trustee of the trust - who is of course the grantor. The trustee is free to manage, invest and spend the trust property as he sees fit for the benefit of the grantor (i.e. himself) and for the benefit of the ultimate beneficiaries of the trust.

As the title to the trust property has been transferred to the trust, the grantor will not be deemed to own any of that trust property in his individual name. As a result, none of these assets will form part of his estate for probate purposes. Instead, when the grantor dies, the person named as 'successor trustee' in the trust agreement will be empowered to distribute the proceeds of the trust to the beneficiaries named in the trust agreement.

We will discuss the settlement of a trust in more detail in Chapter 12. For the moment, you simply need to be aware that assets held in a living trust will not form part of the deceased's estate and will therefore not need to go through probate.

Lifetime Gifts

While it may well go without saying, any property given away during the life of the deceased will not need to go through probate.

Probate Free Transfers of Assets

In some states, like New Jersey, ownership of vehicles which are solely owned by the deceased at the time of death may be transferred immediately to the deceased's surviving spouse/partner or next of kin without the need for probate. Such vehicles include trucks, motor homes and boats provided the total value of the vehicle in question does not exceed the amount specified under state law for such transfers. In most cases that amount will vary between $25,000 and $75,000 (depending on the laws of the deceased's state of residence).

The state's department of motor vehicles can tell you whether the vehicles can be transferred without the need for probate and what needs to be done in order to carry out the transfer. Once you are in a position to legally transfer the vehicle (whether before or after probate as the case may be) the department will, on presentation of a copy of the deceased's death certificate, transfer the title of the vehicle to the relevant beneficiary.

Not all states allow for the transfer of vehicles while probate of the deceased's estate is still on-going. As such, if this option is available you may need to have the vehicle transferred prior to probate or wait until it has concluded.

In addition to vehicles, any salary, wages, accumulated vacation and sick benefits, plus any other fringe benefits, may according to the laws of certain states be paid to a deceased's surviving spouse/partner, adult children or next of kin without the need for probate. The department of labor should be able to tell you whether these procedures apply in the deceased's state and, if so, the deceased's employer should be able to assist you with the process generally. If you are in any doubt as to your rights or those of the beneficiaries of the deceased's estate, or if you are having difficulties extracting the monies from the deceased's employer, you should contact an attorney licensed in the relevant state.

If, for whatever reason, the vehicle or wages (as the case may be) are not transferred before probate commences, the assets may be deemed to form part of the deceased's estate and will need to go through probate. The problem with allowing this is that the spouse or next of kin may not be the beneficiaries of these items under the deceased's will. As such, they may have lost a valuable opportunity to acquire these assets and reduce the size of the probatable estate

– and the related costs of probate which tend to be based on the values of the probatable estate. As such, any such transfers should preferably be made at the earliest opportunity following the deceased's death.

 Sample Form

Sample Form to Transfer a Motor Vehicle – State of New Jersey

(This form is used to transfer an automobile that is jointly owned between husband and wife)

STATE OF NEW JERSEY

DEPARTMENT OF LAW AND PUBLIC SAFETY

DIVISION OF MOTOR VEHICES

AFFIDAVIT

I, _____ undersigned, certify that I am the surviving spouse of _____.

The deceased's name,_____,
and my name,_____,
appear on the certificate of ownership number _____
as follows:_____
_____

I further certify that from the time my name and the deceased's name appeared on the certificate of ownership number

-_____until the death of the deceased on
_____, our relationship was husband and wife.

x_____

(L.S.)

Sworn and subscribed to before me on

_____

_____

Notary Public of New Jersey

CHAPTER 8:

HOW TO INITIATE THE PROBATE PROCESS

Chapter Overview

In this chapter, we will examine the different types of probate procedure that can be used to wind up the deceased's estate; as well as how to initiate the probate process.

Chapter 8

CHAPTER 8

HOW TO INITIATE THE PROBATE PROCESS

What are the Main Steps in a Probate?

Generally speaking, there are three specific steps in every probate proceeding:-

1. the opening of probate;

2. the provision of notice to creditors and the administration of the deceased's estate; and

3. the closing of probate.

A probate is opened by filing a petition in the probate court for the purpose of (i) having the deceased's last will & testament validated and admitted to probate and (ii) appointing an executor to administer the deceased's estate. If the probate is to be carried out formally, that is under the supervision of the probate court, there will be a brief court hearing in order to formally commence the probate of the deceased's estate. However, if the estate is suitable for informal, unsupervised probate no court hearing will be needed. We look at both formal and informal administrations in more detail below.

Once probate has commenced, the next major step is the publication of a notice in a local newspaper calling for creditors of the deceased to present their claims against the estate to the executor within a specific time frame. If a creditor fails to present his claim within the stated time frame, his claim will become statute barred and unenforceable against the deceased's estate. During this notice period, the executor will generally be busy collecting in the assets of the estate and managing them.

Once the creditors' notice period has expired, the creditors' claims paid and the estate administered, the executor will distribute the remainder of deceased's estate to the beneficiaries named in his will or, where no valid will was made, to his heirs in accordance with state intestacy laws. Once these distributions have been made, the executor will close off the estate by filing the necessary documents with the probate court. In the same way as the opening, the closing can be formal or informal. Where the closing is formal, a court hearing will be required. On the other hand, if the closing is informal, no hearing will be required.

Who Can File the Petition?

A representative acting on behalf of the deceased will need to submit an original copy of the deceased's will to the county probate court and file a petition to have that will admitted to probate and the deceased's estate wound up. This representative will usually be the person named as executor in the deceased's will. If the named executor declines to act as executor, any alternate executor named in the will becomes entitled to make the application. If no such person is named or steps forward to carry out the role, the following people will, in the following order, usually have the right to petition the court to have the deceased's estate probated - (1) the deceased's spouse, provided he or she is a beneficiary under the deceased's will, (2) another beneficiary under the deceased's will, (3) the deceased's surviving spouse even if he or she is not a beneficiary under the will, (4) other heirs-at-law of the deceased and (5) creditors of the deceased's estate.

If, on the other hand, the deceased failed to make a will, somebody will need to petition the court to be appointed as administrator of his estate. Once appointed, the administrator will carry out a role which is virtually identical to that carried out by an executor. The priority in which people are entitled to apply to the court to be appointed as administrator is set out under state intestacy law (see Chapter 4). In most cases, the person that ends up being appointed as administrator is the surviving spouse or adult child of the deceased. However, if there is any dispute over who should be entitled to serve as administrator, the probate court has discretion to determine who will be appointed and even has the power to appoint an independent public administrator to assume the role if it deems fit.

Where to File a Petition for Probate

Generally, the state in which the deceased lived and maintained a permanent residence at the time of his death will be the state in which his estate is probated. It follows that it will be the laws of that state which govern the administration and taxation of the deceased's estate.

Important Note

The probate court in the state in which the deceased was 'domiciled' will have jurisdiction over the probate of all of the deceased's personal property and all real estate located in that state.

While the question of permanent residence seems like a straightforward test, the determination of permanent residence can be complex where the deceased resided in more than one place. Where a question arises as to where the deceased permanently resided, the court will look to see where the deceased was 'domiciled'. A person's domicile is the place where he considers himself or herself to be from, the place to which he or she always intended to return or remain. While it is beyond the scope of this book to fully examine the concept of domicile, there are a number of key indicators which serve to identify where a person is domiciled. For example, it will usually be the place where the person in question spends most of his or her time, where his or her family resides, where he or she is registered to vote, etc.

The determination as to which state the testator was domiciled in at the time of his death is of fundamental importance as it directly affects the manner in which his estate will be distributed and the taxation of his estate. By way of simple example, in certain states a spouse has a legal right to choose between the gifts left to him in his spouse's will or to take a defined portion of his deceased spouse's estate. Naturally, if he was left very little under the terms of his deceased spouse's will he would be inclined, in the case of a conflict as to where the deceased spouse resided, to assert that his deceased spouse resided in the state which would give him the greater share of his deceased spouse's estate. The same concept applies with taxes – naturally the surviving beneficiaries of the deceased would, in the case of conflict, seek to assert that the deceased was domiciled in the state which would apply the least taxes to the estate and, more importantly, their inheritances.

Ancillary Probate

While the probate court in the state in which the deceased was domiciled (the "home state") will have jurisdiction over (i) all of the deceased's personal property and (ii) all of the deceased's real estate located in that state, it will have no jurisdiction in relation to real estate held outside that state as state laws only govern the transfer of real estate located in that state.

If the deceased owned real estate in a state other than the home state, it will be necessary to carry out an ancillary or secondary probate administration in that other state (the "ancillary state") in order to deal with that piece of real estate. Of course if the real estate can be transferred by a 'small estate' procedure in the ancillary state, a second or ancillary probate may not be necessary.

An ancillary probate proceeding is a scaled-back proceeding that relates only to assets located in a particular state. In most cases, the courts in the ancillary state will accept the will admitted to probate in the deceased's home state and will issue letters of authority to the executor to enable him or her to transfer the property to the beneficiary named in the deceased's will – or if there was no will, to the deceased's heirs-at-law.

As a matter of procedure, the deceased's will is first administered by the courts of the home state. Once this is done, ancillary proceedings can begin in the ancillary state or states in which the deceased owned additional real estate (including land). Assuming that the will named beneficiaries for each piece of real estate located in the ancillary state, the property will go to the named beneficiaries irrespective of which state the property is situated in or by which probate court the administration is handled.

While the probate process will take additional time where the deceased owned real estate in a number of states, a properly drafted will and an experienced probate lawyer can ensure the smooth transfer of the property to the deceased's beneficiaries. However, if the deceased failed to leave a will or left a will which failed to dispose of the property located in an ancillary state, the intestate administration laws of that ancillary state will determine the heirs-at-law who will be entitled to the property.

In relation to executors, it should be noted that while the ancillary state courts may accept the will admitted to probate in the home state, they may also require the appointment of an executor who is resident in the ancillary state. Alternatively, they may accept an executor who is resident outside the ancillary state, but in doing so may impose specific restrictions or requirements on that executor before formally allowing them to probate the assets located in that ancillary state (see Chapter 1 which refers to the position in respect of out-of-state executors). This of course is likely to have further cost implications for the estate.

Finally, in the same way that the ancillary state's probate laws apply to real estate located in that state, so too will the tax laws. In essence, this means that any inheritance or state taxes due in respect of the probate of the real property in the ancillary state will be payable to the ancillary state and not to the home state.

How Long Will Probate Take?

The time taken for probate varies from state to state and from case to case. While many probates take less than a year, the actual time required depends on a variety of factors including:-

- the notice period within which creditors are obliged to file claims against the estate;

- the extent, value and type of property owned by the deceased;

- how quickly the executor acts in opening and administering the probate process;

- whether the probate is formal or informal; and

- whether the deceased's beneficiaries/heirs dispute the executor's decisions or handling of the estate or even the deceased's will.

Is a Lawyer Required to Assist With Probate?

Whether or not you will need a lawyer to assist you in dealing with the probate will depend on the complexity of the deceased's estate, the type of probate proceeding taking place and the laws of the home/ancillary state. For instance, certain states permit only lawyers to conduct legal proceedings. Therefore, you will need a lawyer if any court hearings are scheduled to take place as part of the probate proceedings.

However, for administering a small estate or for carrying out an unsupervised probate, which account for over half of all probates in the United States, there should be no need to appoint a lawyer provided of course that you are both comfortable enough and diligent enough to learn about the process on your own. Most county probate courts have guides which set out the specific requirements which need to be adhered to in the carrying out a probate in that particular county. We recommend that you contact the county probate court to obtain a copy of any such guide before commencing the probate process.

If you choose to deal with the probate yourself, you will be able to get assistance from the court clerk from time to time along the way. However, it is important to remember that most probate registrars or court clerks are not attorneys. As such their role is one of mere guidance, not the provision of specific advice. As such, if you come to an impasse in respect of a particular decision, you may need to turn to an attorney for advice.

Types of Probate

Before commencing the probate of an estate, you will need to decide on the most suitable type of probate administration for that estate. In this regard, you will generally have three specific options to choose from including:

    (i)   small estate administration;

    (ii) unsupervised administration; and

    (iii) supervised administration.

152 | HOW TO PROBATE AN ESTATE - A STEP-BY-STEP GUIDE FOR EXECUTORS

The availability of each option will depend on state law and the size of the deceased's estate. The type of probate administration chosen is very important as it will have a direct impact on the level of costs and time incurred in probating the estate. If you are in any doubt as to which option is the best for the estate in the circumstances, you should speak to an attorney licensed in the deceased's state of residence.

Small Estate Administration

The laws in most states allow for the transfer of 'small estates' in a simple, cheap and efficient manner outside of the main probate process. While the definition of a 'small estate' varies from state to state, it can be generally defined as an estate:

(i)   which has a total value below a certain financial amount; and/or

(ii) in which the bulk of the estate assets will be either transferred by operation of law to the surviving family members of the deceased or used to pay the debts associated with the deceased's last illness.

Where an estate is deemed to be a 'small estate' for the purposes of state law, it will normally be possible to transfer the assets comprising the small estate to the deceased's heirs using one of two streamlined transfer procedures. These procedures include a 'small estate affidavit' procedure and a 'summary administration' procedure. In some states both procedures will be available while in others only one of the procedures will be available. We look at each below.

Small Estate Affidavit

Where the estate of a deceased person qualifies as a small estate, one or more of the beneficiaries (the "applicant") will usually be able to claim ownership and possession of the deceased's assets from third parties by simply completing a "small estate" affidavit and presenting it to the third party.

In completing the affidavit, the applicant will need to set out details of the identities of any other claimants, beneficiaries or heirs that may have a right to receive part of the deceased's estate. Once completed, the affidavit will need to be signed and sworn by the applicant in the presence of a notary in the state in which it is to be filed. Once notarized, the applicant will file the affidavit with the probate court at which time it becomes a legal document.

If any potential claimants have been identified in the small estate affidavit, the applicant may be obliged to notify them that he has filed a small estate affidavit in respect of the deceased's property and that he intends to use it to take possession and ownership of that property. This advance notification allows potential claimants a period of time in which to take appropriate steps, if necessary, to challenge the applicant's right to do so. Assuming that the notice period expires and no challenges are made, the affidavit can be presented to third parties who will be legally obliged to transfer the ownership and possession of the deceased's assets to the applicant upon presentation.

> An affidavit is a sworn declaration that is filed with the court.

There are however limitations in terms of when the small estate affidavit procedure can be used.

Firstly, the small estate affidavit procedure will only be capable of being used in a particular state where the combined value of all of the deceased's property in that state (excluding property that passes outside of probate and property located in other states), less liens and encumbrances, is less than a certain threshold value. This value varies from state to state up to a maximum of approximately $140,000.

Important Note: Finding Forms

Small estate affidavits usually come in the form of fill-in-the-blank type forms. These forms can normally be obtained from your local probate court or from the probate court's website. If the forms are not available there, you can refer to your state's probate code as the code usually contains a sample of the form of affidavit required. If there is no sample form available, you can prepare your own affidavit based on the requirements set out in the probate code although it's perhaps best to have a lawyer do so.

Secondly, the small estate affidavit can generally only be used to collect certain types of property including unpaid wages, the proceeds of bank accounts, cars, boats, certificates of deposit, stocks and bonds. Generally, real property cannot be collected using a small estate affidavit. However, the laws in California, Nebraska and Texas allow the collection of real property using an affidavit provided the value of the property is under a certain threshold.

Thirdly, each state sets down a specific period of time which must elapse before the small estate affidavit procedure can be used. This period can be between 10 to 180 days from the date of the deceased's death, although 30 to 60 days is most common. This is to allow for challenges to the applicant's right to collect the deceased's assets and for an executor to commence formal proceedings if more suitable in the circumstances.

Finally, certain states place limitations on who can use the procedure and some even limit the procedure to use by a spouse or child of the deceased. As such, you will need to check with the local probate court to see whether you (as executor) will be entitled to avail of the small affidavit procedure. If not, you may consider encouraging the deceased's spouse or children to use the procedure.

A sample "small estate affidavit" form is contained on the next page.

Sample Form

Sample Affidavit for Collection of Personal Property of Deceased - State of Alaska

AFFIDAVIT FOR COLLECTION OF PERSONAL PROPERTY OF DECEASED

I, [   ], being duly sworn, state the following:

1.   I am the successor of _____who died on _____, 20__. I am the successor by reason of the fact that (state basis upon which you claim to be successor).

2.   The entire estate of the deceased, wherever located, less liens and encumbrances, consists only of not more than

        a. vehicles subject to registration under AS 28.10.011 with a total value that does not exceed $100,000; and

        b. personal property, other than vehicles described in (a) above, that does not exceed $50,000.

3.   The deceased's estate includes no real estate.

4.   Thirty days have elapsed since the death of the deceased.

5.   No application or petition for the appointment of an executor of the deceased's estate is pending or has been granted in any jurisdiction.

6.   I, as successor of the deceased, am entitled to the payment of any sums of money due and owing to the deceased and to the delivery of all tangible personal property belonging to the deceased and to the delivery of all instruments evidencing a debt, obligation, stock or chose in action belonging to the deceased.

7.   I understand that when I receive the deceased's assets, I am accountable for them to any executor of the estate (if one is appointed) and to any other person who has a superior right. AS 13.16.685

8.   I understand I may be asked to show a copy of the deceased's death certificate to the holder of the property before any property is transferred to me.

Signature   _____

Mailing Address   _____

City state ZIP   _____

Telephone   _____

Subscribed and sworn to or affirmed before me at _____, Alaska on (date).

(SEAL) Notary Public or other person authorized to administer oaths.

My commission expires:_____

Alaska Statutes

Sec. 13.06.050. General definitions

(48) "successor" means a person, other than a creditor, who is entitled to property of a deceased under the deceased's will or AS 13.06 - AS 13.36;

Sec. 13.16.680. Collection of personal property by affidavit.

(a) Thirty days after the death of a deceased, any person indebted to the deceased or having possession of tangible personal property or an instrument evidencing a debt, obligation, stock, or chose in action belonging to the deceased shall make payment of the indebtedness or deliver the tangible personal property or an instrument evidencing a debt, obligation, stock, or chose in action to a person claiming to be the successor of the deceased upon being presented an affidavit made by or on behalf of the successor stating that

(1)   the entire estate, wherever located, less liens and encumbrances, consists only of not more than

(A) vehicles subject to registration under AS 28.10.011 with a total value that does not exceed $100,000; and

(B) personal property, other than vehicles described in (A) of this paragraph that does not exceed $50,000;

(2) 30 days have elapsed since the death of the deceased;

(3) no application or petition for the appointment of a executor is pending or has been granted in any jurisdiction; and

(4) the claiming successor is entitled to payment or delivery of the property.

(b) A transfer agent of any security shall change the registered ownership on the books of a corporation from the deceased to the successor or successors upon the presentation of an affidavit as provided in (a) of this section. (§ 1 ch 78 SLA 1972; am § 4 ch 80 SLA 1984)

Sec. 13.16.685. Effect of affidavit.

The person paying, delivering, transferring, or issuing personal property or the evidence of it under affidavit is discharged and released to the same extent as if the person dealt with an executor of the deceased. The person is not required to see to the application of the personal property or evidence of it or to inquire into the truth of any statement in the affidavit. If any person to whom an affidavit is delivered refuses to pay, deliver, transfer, or issue any personal property or evidence of it, it may be recovered or its payment, delivery, transfer, or issuance compelled upon proof of their right in a proceeding brought for the purpose by or on behalf of the persons entitled to it. Any person to whom payment, delivery, transfer, or issuance is made is answerable and accountable for it to any executor of the estate or to any other person having a superior right. (§ 1 ch 78 SLA 1972)

Sec. 28.10.011. Vehicles subject to registration.

Every vehicle driven, moved, or parked upon a highway or other public parking place in the state shall be registered under this chapter except when the vehicle is

(1) driven or moved on a highway only for the purpose of crossing the highway from one private property to another, including an implement of husbandry as defined by regulation;

(2) driven or moved on a highway under a dealer's plate or temporary permit as provided for in AS 28.10.031 and 28.10.181(j);

(3) special mobile equipment as defined by regulation;

(4)   owned by the United states;

(5)   moved by human or animal power;

(6)   exempt under 50 U.S.C. App. 501-591 (Soldiers' and Sailors' Civil Relief Act);

(7)   driven or parked only on private property;

(8)   the vehicle of a non-resident as provided under AS 28.10.121;

(9)   transported under a special permit under AS 28.10.151;

(10)   being driven or moved on a highway, vehicular way, or a public parking place in the state that is not connected by a land highway or vehicular way to

    (A)   the land-connected state highway system; or

    (B)   a highway or vehicular way with an average daily traffic volume greater than 499;

(11)   an implement of husbandry operated in accordance with the provisions of AS 19.10.065;

(12)   an electric personal motor vehicle

Summary Administration

A summary administration is similar in ways to the small estate affidavit process set out above save that (i) it is a streamlined version of a full traditional probate and (ii) usually relates to slightly larger estates.

In order to qualify for a summary administration, the deceased's estate must be worth less than a threshold amount determined by the probate laws of the state in which he was resident at the time of his death. These threshold values currently range as high as $200,000 in some states. In determining the value of the estate, real estate may or may not be included depending on the laws of the state in question. This of course can have a significant impact in determining whether the summary administration procedure can be used or not.

While the law varies from state to state, certain states require that the deceased's creditors be paid from the deceased's assets before the summary procedure can be used to distribute assets. You will need to check with the probate court as to the laws which apply in the state in which the probate is taking place.

Important Note

Small estate administrations vary from state to state and you will find that each state has different costs, timelines, rules, forms and regulations. Therefore, if you have any questions regarding any aspect of the small estate procedure, you should speak to the probate court clerk or a lawyer licensed in the state in which the probate is taking place.

General

To find out the correct procedure in your state for administering small estates, you should telephone the probate court and ask the clerk for the necessary form for applying for administering a small estate. These forms are also often available on the internet for download (see your local/state court's website) and usually contain details of the precise process to be followed. Once you obtain the form, you can fill it out, have it notarized where necessary and file it together with the deceased's death certificate and the nominal fee at the court office in order to apply to have you (or another family member of the deceased) appointed as executor of the estate. In some cases you will need to have the spouse and/or children sign their consent to your request to be appointed executor.

Once you have been authorized by the court to act as executor of the deceased's estate, you can approach financial institutions holding the deceased's assets and request that they transfer the assets to the relevant beneficiaries. In most cases, the financial institutions will require sight of your letters of authority as issued by the probate court as well as a copy of the deceased's death certificate.

The important point about this procedure is that there is often no obligation to give notice to creditors to make claims against the estate. As such, you can quickly distribute the estate assets and close the estate. You may, however, be required to use the probate assets obtained through the small estate procedure to pay the creditors of the estate, so check the laws of your state to make certain as the laws do vary from state to state.

Sample Form

Sample Small Estate Affidavit – State of Washington

STATE OF WASHINGTON

Estate of:

_____

_____   Small Estate Affidavit

_____   (RCW 11.62.010)

_____

_____ Deceased.

Having been sworn under oath, I declare as follows:

1. Deceased's Death Certificate. A copy of Deceased's Death Certificate is attached to this Affidavit.

2. Forty-Days Since Death. Forty (40) or more days have elapsed since Deceased's death.

3. Washington Resident. Deceased was a resident of Washington at his/ her death.

4. No Executor. No application or petition for the appointment of an Executor is pending or has been granted in any jurisdiction.

5. Deceased's Net Probate Estate Does Not Exceed $100,000. The value of Deceased's entire estate subject to probate, not including any surviving spouse's community property interest in such assets, wherever located, less liens and encumbrances, does not exceed one-hundred thousand dollars ($100,000).

6. Deceased's Debts. All of Deceased's debts, including funeral and burial expenses, have been paid or provided for.

7. My Name & Address. My name and address are as shown below.

8. Claiming Successor. I am a "successor" of Deceased as defined in RCW 11.62.005.

9. Other Claiming Successors.

[ ] No Others. I am the only claiming Successor; there are no others.

OR

[ ] Other Claiming Successors. There are other claiming Successors. I have given each of them written notice, by personal service or mail, identifying my claim and describing the property claimed. At least ten (10) days have elapsed since the service or mailing of such notice

10. Entitlement to Property.

[ ] Sole Entitlement. I am personally entitled to full payment or delivery of the property claimed.

OR

[ ] Entitlement on Behalf of All Claiming Successors. I am personally entitled to full payment or delivery of the property claimed on behalf and with the written authority, of all other claiming Successors; a copy of which authority is attached to this Affidavit.

11. Property Claimed. A description of the personal property claimed, all of which is subject to probate, is as follows:

Dated: _____

Signature: _____

Deceased's Claiming Successor

Printed Name: _____

Address: _____

_____

_____STATE OF WASHINGTON)

) ss.

COUNTY OF _____)

SUBSCRIBED AND SWORN TO before me this _____ day of _____, 20____ .

_____

Signature

_____

Printed Name

NOTARY PUBLIC for Washington

Residing at: _____

My appointment expires on: _____

Declaration under Penalty of Perjury

I declare under penalty of perjury under the laws of the state of Washington that the following is true and correct to the best of my knowledge:

1.   Name & Address. My name and address are as shown below.

2.   Receipt of Small Estate Affidavit. I have received a copy of the Small Estate Affidavit dated, in which the Claimant declares that he/she is a Claiming Successor of the Deceased.

3.   Claiming Successor. I am also a "successor" of Deceased as defined in RCW 11.62.005.

4.   Authorization. I authorize the Claimant to receive full payment or delivery of the property claimed on my behalf.

5.   Accounting. I am providing this authorization to the Claimant in consideration of his/her promise to me that he/she will account to me for all payments or deliveries of property received under his/her Small Estate Affidavit within five (5) business days of its receipt. This Paragraph 5 concerns the rights and liabilities between only the Claimant and me. No possessor of any property claimed has any responsibility to see to the application of any property transferred to the Claimant.

SIGNED

Date: On   _____

Place: At   _____

Signature: _____

                       Another Claiming Successor of Deceased

Printed Name: _____

Address: _____

                       _____

Small Estates with High Debt Levels

Generally speaking, if the deceased did not have any or much property to transfer, formal probate would not be necessary and one of the more simplified procedures could be used. However, the deceased's relatives may nonetheless decide to conduct formal probate proceedings where the deceased died owing high levels of debts and/or taxes. This is done for the purpose of ensuring a proper windup of the deceased's estate and ensuring that creditors' claims (if any) can be properly dealt with.

With formal probate, creditors are allocated a specific time frame within which to notify the estate of any claims that they might have against it. If a creditor fails to serve the appropriate notice within the time allocated under state law, their claim becomes statute barred. This means that the creditor will lose the right to claim against the estate if notice of the claim is not served within the allocated time frame. If it is proposed to probate an estate for these specific reasons, it is advisable to speak to an attorney to ascertain the best options available in the circumstances.

Unsupervised Administration

An unsupervised probate proceeding is generally available in states that have adopted the Uniform Probate Code. Like summary administrations, it is a simplified and cheaper method of probating an estate – particularly when compared to the supervised probate process (discussed below).

An unsupervised probate procedure typically involves filing forms with the probate court, having the probate court approve the appointment of someone to wind up the deceased's estate (this may not necessarily be the executor named in the deceased's will), paying any debts and taxes owing by the estate, distributing the deceased's assets to the beneficiaries named in his will and, finally, if required, having the court approve those distributions. In most instances, there will be no formal hearing or court supervision and the court's role is reduced to one of simply reviewing the paperwork filed.

 Important Note

The most significant advantage of unsupervised probate is that it reduces the delays usually associated with finalizing and distributing the estate by eliminating audit and accounting reviews by the court.

The unsupervised probate process can be used for estates that exceed the monetary limits set out for small estate administration but nonetheless don't require a large degree of supervision by the courts to facilitate an orderly wind up. This would generally be the case where the estate does not have high debt levels, where there are no challenges to the deceased's will and where there are no disputes in relation to the validity of the deceased's will.

The majority of states currently have procedures for unsupervised probate administration – particularly states that have adopted the Uniform Probate Code. The original intent behind the introduction of these procedures was to speed up the probate process – which typically lasted a year or so. However, some states only allow unsupervised administration if all interested parties consent in advance to the procedure or if the will allows for it. Yet others, including states which have adopted the Uniform Probate Code, allow the appointed administrator to commence proceedings in this way but reserve a right for interested parties to petition the court to have the proceedings converted to a traditional supervised probate process. In which case, an executor will need to be appointed and the parties will need to go through all the usual formalities associated with supervised probate.

The court has broad discretion to grant a petition for unsupervised probate, even against the deceased's wishes. Unless there is an official objection, most executors will be appointed to administer the estate without the supervision of the court, if they request it.

Factors which could cause the court to decide to temporarily or permanently carry out a formal supervised probate process include objections to the conduct or suitability of the executor, an interested party's wish to have the court review the distribution of the deceased's estate, objections to legal fees or other serious concerns about the manner in which the administration is being conducted.

Despite the fact that the probate is unsupervised, as executor you still need to pay careful attention to the process as your duties as executor will apply as if it was a traditional probate procedure. You will still be acting as a fiduciary (a person in a position or office of trust) and, as such, you will still be held to the same high standards of conduct as would be expected of an executor. In addition, you will still need to prepare a number of documents as part of the probate process. Some will need to be given to interested persons while others will need to be filed with the probate court and tax authorities within very specific time frames. You will also need to keep careful accounting records of everything that you do with the estate in case any challenges are made to convert the procedure to a supervised or formal probate procedure.

In addition, you will still need to place an advertisement in the newspaper calling for creditors to inform the estate of any monies owing to them by the deceased. Similar to supervised probate, the creditors will need to notify you within a specific period of time, as set out under state law, of any debts that may be owing by the deceased' estate.

However, a positive aspect of unsupervised administration is that, in a number of states, there will be no need to obtain the court's approval in relation to the proposed distribution plan for the deceased's assets or in relation to the payment of remuneration to the executor. As well as that, there may be no requirement to prepare and file a final accounting for the estate with the probate court. This means a saving in time and expense for everyone involved.

Sample Form

SUMMARY OF APPLICATION PROCEDURE FOR INFORMAL PROBATE IN ARIZONA

Arizona Statutes require that an executor be appointed to administer the probate. Administration of an estate includes filing a verified statement, publishing notice to creditors, giving notice as required, making distributions, filing receipts, paying taxes and closing the estate according to law.

The forms required in an ordinary probate are set out below:

Testate Estate - (Leaving a valid will)

1. Application for Informal Probate of will and Appointment of Executor **(Form PR-08)**
2. General Order to the Executor
3. statement of Informal Probate of will and Appointment of Executor **(Form PR-12)**
4. Probate Information Sheet **(PR-Cover)**
5. Letters and Acceptance of Executor **(Form PR-14)**
6. Verified statement Pursuant to A.R.S 14-5651 **(Form PR-15)**
7. Notice to Heirs and Devisees of Informal Probate and Appointment - **(Form PR-18)**
8. Notice to Creditors (You need both the forms listed below)
a. For Publication - **(Form PR-80)**
b. To known Creditors - **(Form PR-80A)**
9. Proof of Notice to Known Creditors/statement of no Known Creditors **(PR-80B)**
10. Proof of Mailing/Delivery of Inventory **(Form PR-71)**
11. Instrument or Deed of Distribution **(Form PR-101)**
12. Closing statement (You will need one of the forms listed below)
    Regular Closing statement **(Form PR-114)** or
    a.Summary Administration Closing statement **(Form PR-114A)**

Other forms may be needed in the initial filing of probate. Some of these forms include

1.   Renunciation of:

        a. Right to Appointment

        b. Right to Nominate

        c. Concurrence in Nomination

        d. Waiver of Bond **(Form PR-4)**

2.   Waiver of Bond **(Form PR-5)**

Intestate Estate - (Leaving no will)

1.   Application for Informal Appointment of Executor **(Form PR-9)**

2.   General Order to the Executor

3.   Informal Appointment of Executor **(Form PR-13)**

4.   Probate Information Sheet **(PR-Cover)**

5.   Letters and Acceptance of Executor **(Form PR-14)**

6.   Verified statement Pursuant to A.R.S 14-5651 **(Form PR-15)**

7.   Notice to Heirs of Informal Appointment - Intestate **(Form PR-19)**

8.   Notice to Creditors (You need both the forms listed below)

a.   For Publication - **(Form PR-80)**

b.   To known Creditors - **(Form PR-80A)**

9.   Proof of Notice to Known Creditors/statement of no Known Creditors **(PR-80B)**

10.   Proof of Mailing/Delivery of Inventory **(Form PR-71)**

11.   Instrument or Deed of Distribution **(Form PR-101)**

12.   Closing statement (You will need one of the forms listed below)

.   Regular Closing statement **(Form PR-114)** or

        a. Summary Administration Closing statement **(Form PR-114A)**

Other forms may be needed in the initial filing of probate. Some of these forms include

1.   Renunciation of:

        a. Right to Appointment

        b. Right to Nominate

        c. Concurrence in Nomination

        d. Waiver of Bond **(Form PR-4)**

2.   Waiver of Bond **(Form PR-5)**

* Source: Arizona Superior court in Pima County website (http://www. **sc.pima.gov)**

Formal or Supervised Probate Administration

A supervised probate is the most formal and expensive method of probate. In such procedures, the court plays a very active supervisory role in approving each transaction carried out by the executor. Specifically, the executor must obtain the consent of the court before selling or disposing of any of the estate assets or paying any costs or fees.

In states where it's possible to chose between supervised and unsupervised probate, a court may decide to conduct a supervised probate where:-

- the will is contested;

- an interested party requests it;

- the beneficiaries cannot agree on who should act as executor where none has been named in the will; or

- the executor's ability to carry out the process is in question.

In some states, probate proceedings can be formal in parts and informal in others. For example, the proceedings could start out on a formal basis with a court hearing being convened to appoint an executor. However, the same proceedings could end informally with papers being filed with the court setting out how the estate assets are to be distributed amongst the beneficiaries named in the deceased's will – without the need to have the court approve the distribution plan in advance of making any distributions to the beneficiaries. The precise procedure for opening and closing an estate changes from state to state so you will need to check with your local probate court to confirm the rules in the deceased's state of residence.

Initiating Supervised Probate

One of the first things that should to be done following the death of the deceased is to file a copy of the deceased's will with the probate court. This should be done irrespective of whether formal probate is anticipated or not. In the majority of states, state law will set out particular time frames within which the deceased's will must be filed with the probate court. This usually tends to be within 30 days of its discovery - but the timing does vary slightly from state to state.

Once the will has been filed, the next step in the process will be to file a 'Petition for Probate of Will and Appointment of an Executor'. This filing is made at the probate court clerk's office in the state in which the deceased resided at the time of his death and is usually made by the executor. However, it is open to anyone who has an interest in the estate (beneficiaries of the will, heirs-at-law or creditors) to lodge the petition to commence probate.

The petition for probate of a will is a printed form which is generally available from the probate court, a probate lawyer, on the internet or from stationary suppliers. A sample petition is contained on the next page.

Sample Form

SAMPLE APPLICATION FOR INFORMAL PROBATE OF WILL AND INFORMAL APPOINTMENT OF PERSONAL REPRESENTATIVE IN COLORADO

☐ District court ☐ Denver probate court

_____ County, Colorado

Court Address:

IN THE MATTER OF THE Estate OF:

Deceased

Attorney or Party Without Attorney

_____

_____

_____

_____

Phone Number: _____
E-mail: _____
FAX Number: _____
MAtty. Reg. #: _____

court USE ONLY

Case Number:

_____

Division

courtroom: _____

APPLICATION FOR INFORMAL PROBATE OF WILL AND INFORMAL APPOINTMENT OF PERSONAL REPRESENTATIVE

1. Applicant, (Name) _____ as
    _____, is an interested person. **(§15-10-201, C.R.S.)**
2. The deceased died on the date of _____,
    at the age of _____ years, domiciled in the   City of
    _____, County of _____, state
    of _____.

3. Venue for this proceeding is proper in this county because the deceased:
    ☐ was a domiciliary of this county on the date of death.
    ☐ was not a domiciliary of Colorado, but property of the deceased was located in this county on the date of death.

4. ☐ No personal representative has been appointed by a court in this state or elsewhere.
    ☐ A personal representative of the deceased has been appointed by a court in this state or elsewhere as shown on the attached explanation. **(§15-12-301, C.R.S.)**

5. Applicant:
    ☐ has not received a demand for notice and is unaware of any demand for notice of any probate or appointment proceeding concerning the deceased that may have been filed in this state or elsewhere.

    ☐ has received, or is aware of, a demand for notice. See attached demand or explanation.

6. The date of deceased's last will is _____
    _____. The dates of all codicils are

    _____

    _____.

    The will and any codicils are referred to as the will. The will:
    ☐ was deposited with this court before the deceased's death. **(§15-11-515, C.R.S.)**
    ☐ has been delivered to this court since the deceased's death. **(§15-11-516, C.R.S.)**
    ☐ accompanies this application.
    ☐ has been probated in the state of _____.
    Authenticated copies of the will and of the statement

    probating it accompany this application. **(§15-12-303, C.R.S.)**

7. Except as may be disclosed on an attached explanation and after the exercise of reasonable diligence, applicant is unaware of any instrument revoking the will, is unaware of any prior wills which have

not been expressly revoked by a later instrument and believes that the will is the deceased's last will and was validly executed.

8.   No statutory time limitation applies to the commencement of these proceedings. **(§15-12-108, C.R.S.)**

9.   _____

_____

Name, address and telephone number of the nominee for Personal Representative _____

_____

is 21 years of age or older and has priority for appointment because of:

□ nomination by the will.

□ statutory priority. **(§15-12-203, C.R.S.)**

□ reasons stated in the attached explanation.

Those persons having prior or equal rights to appointment have renounced their rights to appointment or have been given notice of these proceedings. **(§15-12-310, C.R.S.)** Any required renouncements accompany this application.

10.   The nominee is to serve in unsupervised administration and without bond. Bond is not required by the will, nor has bond been demanded by an interested person. **(§§15-12-603 and 605, C.R.S.)**

11.   The deceased □ was □ was not married at time of death.

12.   Listed below are the names and addresses of deceased's spouse, children, heirs and devisees and the names and addresses of guardians or conservators of incapacitated or protected persons. (See instructions below.)

NAME (Include spouse, if any)	ADDRESS (or date of death)	AGE AND DATE OF BIRTH OF MINORS	INTEREST AND RELATIONSHIP (See instructions)

PETITIONER REQUESTS that the court set a time and place of hearing; that notice be given to all interested persons as provided by law; that after notice and hearing, the court determine the heirs of the deceased and formally admit the deceased's will to probate; that the nominee:

    ☐ be formally appointed as personal representative   ☐ be formally confirmed as personal representative

    ☐ without bond   ☐ with bond

    ☐ in unsupervised administration   ☐ in supervised administration (additional fee required)

and that Letters Testamentary be issued to the personal representative or confirmed. Petitioner also requests:

    ☐ a setting aside of prior informal findings as to testacy,

    ☐ a setting aside of prior informal appointment of personal representative,

    ☐_____

_____

_____

Signature of Attorney for Petitioner   Date

_____   _____

Signature of Petitioner   Date

(Type or Print name below) (Type or Print name, address and telephone # below)

INSTRUCTIONS FOR PARAGRAPH 12:

Include any statements of legal disability or other incapacity required by Rule 10, C.R.P.P.

List the names and dates of death of any deceased devisees. (See applicable antilapse statute, §§15-11-601 and 603, C.R.S.)

Where a listed person is an heir, detail the relationship to the deceased which creates heirship. Examples: son, daughter of pre-deceased son.

(§§15-11-101 to 114, C.R.S.)

Attach additional sheets if necessary.

* Source:- Colorado state Judicial Branch, http://www.courts.state.co.us

Notifying Interested Parties of the Hearing

Following the filing of the petition, a date will usually be set for the person named as executor (or administrator) to appear before the probate court, present the will and request that he be formally appointed as executor of the deceased's estate. If you have already filed the original will with the court clerk, presentation of the will may be unnecessary. If you must present the will, the clerk should return it to you upon request before the hearing so that you will have it to hand in court. This date will usually be 30 to 45 days following the filing of the petition.

In advance of the court hearing, copies of the following documents must be sent to all interested persons – (a) the petition, (b) the deceased's will and (c) a written notice specifying the date, time and place of the hearing. Interested persons include all persons or entities (such as churches, charities and other organizations) named in the deceased's will, the executor(s) named in the will and all persons who would be entitled to inherit from the deceased's estate as heirs-at-law under the rules of intestate succession applicable in the deceased's state of residence (even if the deceased left a valid last will).

As the proposed executor, you will be obliged to make reasonable efforts to locate all interested persons. In certain states, if you don't manage to locate an interested person, you will be obliged to file a sworn declaration or affidavit detailing to the court the various steps you took in order to locate that person.

If the deceased is a citizen of a foreign country and he has:

(i)   died without making a will, or

(ii)   made a will but failed to nominate an executor, or

(iii)   under the terms of his will, gifted his property to a non-U.S. citizen,

you will generally need to give notice of the petition to a recognized diplomatic or consular official of the foreign country of which the deceased was a citizen if officials from that country maintain an office in the United States.

Notice of petition will generally be sent by first class mail or by hand to each interested person or entity at least 15 days or more prior to the hearing. This time period varies from state to state so you will need to check out the specific requirements at the local probate court, at the local library or with a local attorney. In most states, there is a specific form of notice (often called a "Notice of Petition to Administer an Estate") which should be used to notify the interested persons of the petition. A copy of the relevant form can be obtained by contacting your local probate court or visiting its website.

In certain states, you will need to have a third party serve the notices on your behalf. Where this form of service is required, and the third party carries out the required services, he will need to subsequently sign a sworn affidavit of service setting out details of the services that he has made. This affidavit will be sworn in the presence of a notary in the usual way and filed with the probate court. There is usually a standard form of affidavit of service to be signed by the third party and it should be obtainable from the local probate court.

Proving a Will and Dealing With Will Contests

Apart from the formal appointment of an executor, the initial hearing will be used as an opportunity to give interested persons the chance to raise any objections that they may have in relation to validity of the deceased's will. These objections are generally founded on assertions that the will is invalid as it:-

- has been superseded by a later will and is therefore not the deceased's last will;

- it was made at a time when the deceased was mentally incompetent and unable to legally make the decisions he purported to make in his will;

- was made by the deceased under duress or undue influence and was therefore not the free act of the testator; or

- is a forgery, either in whole or in part.

If, having reviewed the deceased's will and the circumstances surrounding its making, the court discovers an irregularity of some kind it has the power to deem all or part only of the will invalid. If the entire will is deemed to be invalid, the deceased will be deemed to have died intestate in which case the rules regarding intestate distribution will be applied to determine how the deceased's estate will be divided amongst his heirs.

As the petition hearing is normally a fairly routine procedure, you should be able to attend same without the need to have a lawyer accompany you. However, if the laws of the probate state require lawyers to be present for probate related hearings or if there is a possibility that there will be any form of challenge made to the deceased's will or question raised as to its authenticity by the court, you should ensure that you have a lawyer in attendance with you as he will be better able to navigate and control the process.

If any questions are raised during the hearing in relation to the execution of the will by the deceased, it may be necessary to summon the people who witnessed the deceased execute his will to court in order to have them to testify to that fact. Alternatively, if the deceased and the witnesses executed a 'self-proving affidavit' and same is attached to the deceased's will, the court will usually accept that as evidence that the will has been properly executed.

A 'self-proving affidavit' is a declaration sworn, in front of a notary, by the persons who witnessed the deceased sign his will in which they attest to that fact.

On the other hand, if no objections are filed with the court and the court is satisfied that the deceased's will has been validly executed, it will issue an order "admitting the will to probate" and formally appoint you as executor.

Letters of Authority

Once appointed as executor of the deceased's estate, you will have full authority to deal with that estate. In order to evidence your appointment as executor, the court will issue you with a certified court document called "letters of authority" – which are sometimes referred to as "letters testamentary" in certain states. If the deceased died without having made a valid will, the court will issue "letters of administration" to the administrator of that estate.

Letters of authority are recognized by financial institutions and other third parties as your official authority, as executor, to deal with the deceased's estate. As each financial institution you interact with will most likely want to see and retain a copy of your letters of authority before allowing you to deal with the deceased's estate, you will need to obtain several copies of your letters of authority. The court clerk should be able to assist you in issuing certified copies of your letters of authority.

Sample Form

SAMPLE LETTERS – COLORADO

	COURT USE ONLY
□ District court □ Denver probate court _____ County, Colorado court Address: _____ _____ **IN THE MATTER OF THE Estate OF:** □ **Deceased** □ **Protected Person** □**Minor** □**Ward**	 Case Number: Division: courtroom:

LETTERS

(Name) _____ _was appointed or qualified_
by this court or its Registrar on _____ _(date)_
_as:_

□ Personal Representative. The deceased died on
_____ (date).

□ These are Letters of Administration. (The deceased did not leave a will.)

□ These are Letters Testamentary. (The deceased left a will.)

□ Special Administrator in □ an informal □ a formal proceeding. These are Letters of SpecialAdministration.

□ Conservator. These are Letters of Conservatorship.

□ The protected person is a minor whose date of birth is

_____.

□ Special Conservator.

□ Guardian. These are Letters of Guardianship for:

□ an incapacitated person.

□ a minor whose date of birth is_____

□ Emergency Guardian

(Expires on _____(date), not more than 60 days after appointment per §15 14 312, C.R.S.)

Appointment or qualification is by □court order □ will □ written instrument □

_____

_____

These Letters evidence full authority, except for the following limitations or restrictions, if any:_____

_____

Dated:_____   _____

(Deputy) Clerk or Registrar of court

CERTIFICATION

Certification Stamp   or   Certified to be a true
copy of the original in my

custody and to be in full force
and effect as of:

Dated: _____

_____

(Deputy)Clerk of court

It is worth reminding you at this juncture that once a will has been admitted to probate, it becomes a matter of public record as indeed will all other papers you file with the court in connection with the probate. These papers are open to inspection by any member of the public upon payment of a small fee to the probate court. As such, anyone who is mindful enough to inspect the deceased's will can do so and can determine who stood to inherit under the terms of that will.

The Requirements of a Surety Bond

Before appointing an executor of the deceased's estate, a court will usually require that a surety bond be put in place. A surety bond is an insurance bond that protects the beneficiaries of an estate against any depletion in the value of that estate caused as a result of the wrongdoing or negligence of the executor. The requirement for a bond to be put in place can however be waived if the deceased expressly waived that requirement under the terms of his will or if all of the beneficiaries of the deceased's estate sign a letter of waiver under which they waive the requirement to post the bond. In order for the waiver to be recognized by the court, that letter of waiver will need to be attached to the petition for probate when filed with the court office.

However, even where there has been a waiver of the requirement to post a surety bond, the court may determine that a bond is required if it believes that the circumstances warrant. For example, the courts generally require executors that are resident outside the state in which probate is taking place to file a bond even where the requirement has been validly waived.

Where a bond is required, the amount of the bond will be calculated based on the estimated value of the deceased's estate plus the estimated value of the annual gross income of all of the estate's property. This amount will then be set out in the court order granting probate of the estate. It may be possible for an executor to reduce the cover provided by the bond, and as a result its costs, by requesting that the court limits his authority to dealing with the deceased's personal property only (such that the court's consent is required to deal with real property) or by agreeing to deposit marketable securities and/or cash not required for estate administration into a blocked account that cannot be accessed without the prior approval of the court. You will need to check your local probate rules to see what limitations of this kind (if any) are permitted under the relevant state probate laws.

Once the value of the bond has been determined, it will be stated on the court order granting probate of the estate. The order will usually either appoint a named person as executor subject to first putting a bond in place within a specific timeframe or appoint a person as executor and stipulate that the appointment will be automatically revoked if the bond is not put in place within the required timeframe. Insurance companies or surety companies will normally refuse to issue any form of bond to an executor without first receiving a copy of the relevant court order.

If you are required to put a bond in place or anticipate that you may need to put one in place, you should carefully review the relevant state probate laws so that you can familiarize yourself with the relevant timeframes and requirements in relation to bonds.

Notifying Beneficiaries

Once the deceased's will has been successfully admitted to probate and you have been formally appointed as executor of the deceased's estate, the next step will be to formally notify those involved or interested in the deceased's estate of your appointment. In the normal course, you will notify the actual beneficiaries named in the deceased's will and those potential beneficiaries that may be interested in the deceased's estate (such as the deceased's spouse, children and parents) by recorded mail. Creditors, on the other hand, will usually be notified by placing a legal notice in a local newspaper. We'll discuss more about creditors in the next chapter.

Collecting and Inventorying the Estate's Assets

Once all of the relevant parties have been notified of your appointment as executor and you are in possession of the required letters of authority, the next step in administration process will be the collection and inventorying of the deceased's probate assets. Once this is done, you will need to deal with the payment of any debts and taxes owed by the estate. We'll look at each of these items in turn in the ensuing two chapters.

CREDITOR CLAIMS

Chapter Overview

In most cases, when a person dies, they will leave some form of debt behind them – whether in the form of phone bills, credit cards, loans, mortgages or otherwise. As an executor, you will be responsible for dealing with those debts. In this chapter, we take a look at some of those responsibilities.

Chapter 9

CHAPTER 9

CREDITOR CLAIMS

Dealing with Creditors

For a variety of different reasons, many people die leaving some form of unpaid debt behind them. These unpaid debts generally include smaller debts such as phone bills, personal loans, tax bills, and so on. However, they can also include larger debts such as home loans/mortgages or even contingent liabilities relating to litigation against the deceased. The probate process is designed to ensure that all of these debts are paid in full by the deceased – at least to the extent that there are sufficient assets in the deceased's estate to meet those debts.

This is done by requiring you, as the executor of the deceased's estate, to notify all known and potential creditors of the deceased's death. This notification, which is generally in a format prescribed by state law, is made by placing a notice in a newspaper and/or by sending a written notice to the creditors. The notice will request that all creditors of the deceased submit details to you, as executor, of any debts which may be due and owing to them by the deceased. If a creditor fails to submit details of a debt due to you within the time frame stipulated in the notice, he will lose his right to recover that debt from the deceased's estate. On the other hand, if a creditor submits details of a debt due to him, you will need to review the details relating to that debt and determine whether to discharge or dispute that claim.

There are of course some debts which it will be important for you to discharge as soon as possible. These include mortgage payments, insurance premiums, utility bills and other bills which might cause the estate to lose value if not paid. However, before you make any payments, you will need to determine whether the deceased's estate is solvent or insolvent. As you will have already prepared an inventory of the probate assets, you should have a good idea whether the estate is solvent – that is, whether the value of the assets outweigh the value of the liabilities. If this is clearly the case, you may decide to make those important payments as soon as possible in order to protect the estate. However, the payment of other debts is not something that you should rush into. You should first carefully weigh up the merits of each claim before making any payment.

If the estate is insolvent, then you will need to be very careful in terms of how you proceed as the law sets out a specific priority in which an executor of an insolvent estate must pay the estate's debts (see below for further details).

Remember, as executor, you can be removed from office for improperly diminishing the value of the estate if you discharge debts which ought not to have been discharged in the circumstances.

There is a fairly procedural approach which you should take when dealing with the estate's creditors. This includes the following steps:-

- publishing a probate notice to creditors;

- conducting a review of the deceased's affairs in order to identify his creditors;

- giving each possible creditor actual notice in writing of the time frames within which they can make a claim against the estate;

- determining whether a creditor's claim is lawfully presented; and

- disposing of lawfully presented creditors' claims.

By adhering to the order set out above, you should be best positioned to lawfully deal with the creditors of the estate.

Identification and Notification of Creditors

Having already carried out a review of the deceased's papers and affairs in order to determine the assets and liabilities of the estate, you should have a very good idea of the debts owing by the estate. Therefore, once you have obtained your letters of authority, the first step you should take is to notify all those creditors of the deceased's death and of their right to file a claim against the estate for the recovery of any sums owing to them.

It's very important that you notify the creditors of their rights as soon as possible after being formally appointed. This is because, once you give that notification, creditors of the deceased's estate must file their claims with you within a specific period of time. If they don't, they lose the right to make a claim. From an overall timing perspective, it's therefore important to get this clock ticking as soon as possible.

Important Note

There are two different ways in which a creditor can be notified of the death of the deceased and their right to claim against his estate – by sending a written notice to the creditor or by publishing a notice in a local newspaper.

In many states, the executor is required to send a written notice to all known creditors of the deceased that he is aware of. This written notice, which notifies creditors of the deceased's death and of their entitlement to file a claim against the estate, can be in addition to or in substitution for the requirement to publish a notice in a newspaper. The written notice affords an additional degree of protection to the estate as once a notice is served and the affidavit of service sworn, it will be extremely difficult for a creditor to assert that he was unaware of the deceased's death and the need to file a claim within the required time frames.

A typical form of notice is set out on the next page.

Sample Form

Sample Notice to Creditors by delivery- State of Colorado

	COURT USE ONLY
☐ District court ☐ Denver probate court	
_____ County, Colorado court Address:	
IN THE MATTER OF THE Estate OF	
Deceased: Attorney or Party Without Attorney (Name and Address):	Case Number: Division courtroom
Phone Number: E-mail: FAX Number: Atty. Reg.#:	

NOTICE TO CREDITORS BY MAIL OR DELIVERY

NOTICE TO CREDITORS

All persons having claims against the above-named estate are required to present them to the personal representative or the above-named court on or before

_____*, or be forever barred.

              (date)

_____

Signature of Attorney for/or Personal Representative Date

       Type or Print name, of Attorney _____

                                 _____

                                 _____

           Type or Print name and address of Personal Representative

* Insert the later of the following two dates:

- The date set in the published Notice to Creditors by Publication (Form CPC 21-A).

- The date sixty days from the mailing or other delivery of this notice, but not later than the date one year following the deceased's death (Section 15-12-801, C.R.S.).

CERTIFICATE OF SERVICE

I certify that on (date) _____, a copy of this Notice to Creditors by Mail or Delivery was served on each of the following at the indicated address by:

□ hand delivery
□ certified U.S. mail, postage pre-paid

□ first class U.S. mail, postage pre-paid
□ registered U.S. mail, postage pre-paid

Name and Address

_____

Signature of Person Certifying Service

NOTE: This certificate of service cannot be used in cases where personal service is required or used. Use CPC7-P (Personal Service Affidavit) or CPC8-A (Waiver of Service) for each person required to be served personally.

However, in order to cover the situation where the deceased's personal papers failed to provide sufficient information as to the identity of all his creditors, it is generally required that the executor also publishes a notice of the probate proceedings in a newspaper, along with a general invitation to creditors to submit their claims to the executor within the relevant claims period set out under state law. This notice, which is often required to be published for a number of consecutive weeks, should not of course be published until you have been officially appointed as executor and received your letters of authority – otherwise, you run the risk that the notice will be deemed invalid. In which case you will have to repeat the process all over again and probate could be substantially delayed.

 Did You Know?

Publishing a probate notice to creditors immediately following your appointment as executor allows you to substantially reduce the timeframe within which a creditor can take a claim against the deceased's estate. The 'clock' only stops ticking on the date set out in the notice. The longer it takes to issue the notice, the longer it will take for that specific end date to arrive as a specific number of days must elapse between the date of publishing and the end date.

While the laws vary from state to state, the general requirement is that the newspaper notice is placed in at least one newspaper which is in general circulation in the county in which the probate proceedings are being held. A sample notice is set out on the next page.

Remember, the notice to creditors will also need to be filed with the probate court.

Sample Form

Sample Notice to Creditors by publication - State of Colorado	
☐ District court ☐ Denver probate court _____ _ County, Colorado court Address:	COURT USE ONLY Case Number: Division courtroom
IN THE MATTER OF THE Estate OF Deceased Attorney or Party Without Attorney (Name and Address): Phone Number: E-mail: FAX Number: Atty. Reg. #:	
NOTICE TO CREDITORS BY PUBLICATION	

NOTICE TO CREDITORS*

Estate of _____

_____, Deceased

Case Number _____

All persons having claims against the above-named estate are required to present them to the personal representative or to

☐ ☐ District court of _____,
County, Colorado,
☐ ☐ probate court of the City and County of Denver, Colorado**-
on or before (date) _____***, or the
claims may be forever barred.

_____

_____

_____

_____

Type or Print name and address of Personal Representative

* Publish only this portion of the form.
INSTRUCTIONS TO THE NEWSPAPER:

_____

Name of Newspaper

_____   _____

Signature of Attorney for/or Personal Representative   Date

Publish the above Notice to Creditors once
a week for three consecutive calendar weeks

_____

Type or Print name of Attorney for Personal Representative

 **Check whichever court applies.

***Insert date not earlier than four months from the date of first publication or the date one year from date of deceased's death, whichever occurs first

NOTE: Unless one year or more has elapsed since the death of the deceased, a personal representative shall cause a notice to creditors to be published in some daily or weekly newspaper published in the county in which the estate is being administered, or if there is no such newspaper, then in some newspaper of general circulation in an adjoining county. (§15-12-801, C.R.S.) A copy of this form and the Proof of Publication should be filed with the Clerk of the court.

Time Limitations on Submission of Claims

As mentioned, the probate rules of virtually all states require an executor to publish, in a newspaper circulating in the county in which probate is being carried out, a notice of his appointment together with an invitation to creditors of the deceased person's estate to file their claims against the estate with the executor. This publication is treated as sufficient notice to unidentified creditors of the deceased's death and their entitlement to claim against the deceased's estate. More importantly however, it starts the clock ticking on the state's official claim period.

Depending upon the state in which the probate procedure is taking place, creditors of the deceased will have anywhere from three to twelve months following the date of publication of the notice to file a claim with the estate (i.e. with you as executor) or with the probate court (depending on state law). Any claim that is notified after this period has elapsed will become statute barred and will be unenforceable by the creditor.

In the ordinary course, where a creditor files a claim following the expiry of the claim period, the executor is not required to discharge the claim. However, in certain states, the probate court has the authority to extend the claim period in exceptional circumstances; and in some instances can extend it up to three years. As such, it would be sensible to take the advice of an attorney where you are seeking to deny a late claim from a creditor.

Evaluation of Claims

Ordinarily, having previously reviewed the deceased's papers, it should be a relatively straightforward task for you to identify the deceased's creditors and the amounts owing to them – especially where you have clear records of these debts. However, matters can become more complicated where you are notified of a claim by a creditor who is not listed in the deceased's records or where a known creditor files a claim for an amount which is different to that stated in the deceased's records. In such circumstances, you will need to examine the merits of the claim very carefully least of all because you could be held personally liable if you pay out invalid claims or if the creditors are not paid properly.

Due in part to the risk of personal liability, you will need to carefully evaluate every single claim against the deceased's estate in order to determine whether the claim is valid or not – no exceptions. Where you believe the claim to be valid, you can approve the payment of the debt – but only after you have determined whether the estate is solvent or insolvent and, if the latter is the case, applied the rules of priority set out below.

If you do not believe the claim to be valid based on good reason, you can disallow the claim (or part of it) by filing a notice of objection or disallowance (the name of this notice varies from state to state) with the probate court. It is also open to any interested person (e.g. beneficiaries or heirs-at-law) to file such a notice. You will need to complete this form in order to register the objection. The form usually identifies the creditor and sets out details of the reasons for rejecting the claim – whether in whole or in part. The probate court will be able to advise you of the correct form to use. A sample form for the state of Colorado is set out later in this chapter.

In addition, you will also need to send a copy of the notice of objection to the creditor by registered post. Invariably, this will result in litigation against you in your capacity as executor of the estate as the creditor will, in the absence of your agreement, have no other means of recovering against the estate. In which case, you may need to engage the services of an attorney licensed in the state in which the probate is taking place to assist the estate in the defense of any such claims.

Sample Form

Sample Notice of Disallowance of Claim - State of Colorado	
☐ District court ☐ Denver probate court	**COURT USE ONLY**
County, Colorado	
Court Address:	
IN THE MATTER OF THE ESTATE OF:	
Deceased:	
Attorney or Party Without Attorney (Name and Address):	Case Number:
	Division:
Phone Number: E-mail:	Courtroom:
FAX Number: Atty. Reg.#:	
NOTICE OF DISALLOWANCE OF CLAIM	

TO: _____, Claimant:
       Name

The undersigned, as Personal Representative of this estate, disallows

      ☐ all of your claim

      ☐ $ _____ of your claim for $

_____ presented on

_____. (Date)

Failure to protest any disallowance by filing a Petition for Allowance or commencing a proceeding within sixty days after the mailing of this Notice shall result in your claim or the disallowed portion being forever barred.

_____

Type or Print name of Attorney for Personal Representative

_____   _____

Signature of Personal Representative or Attorney   Date

_____

_____

_____

_____

Type or Print name, address & tele. # of Personal Representative

CERTIFICATE OF MAILING

I certify that I mailed a true copy of the above Notice of Disallowance of Claim to
_____ Name

Claimant, on _____ (Date) by depositing it in the United
states Mail, postage prepaid, addressed as follows:

_____

_____

_____

_____

Signature of Person Certifying Service

Similar to the requirement for creditors to notify the estate of claims, all objections against creditors' claims must also be filed with the probate court within a specific time frame for it to be effective. This time frame, while varying from state to state, tends to be between three to four months or, alternatively, within a specific numbers of days following the submission by a creditor of the particular claim. Again, you will need to check the laws of the deceased's state of residence to confirm the time frames applicable in that state. Alternatively, the probate court should be able to assist you.

Payment of Claims in Solvent Estates

Once you have determined which claims are valid claims and the value of those claims, you will need to see whether there are sufficient assets to discharge these debts. If there are sufficient assets to cover the debts, the estate is said to be solvent. Where the estate is solvent you can proceed to pay the debts – but only after the creditors' claim period has expired. However, if there are insufficient liquid assets (i.e. cash) to pay the debts, you may need to sell some of the estate's assets in order to raise the money. This process is known as abatement. Unless the terms of the deceased's will specify otherwise, the laws of the state in which the probate is being carried out will determine the order in which the deceased's estate is to be abated. A typical abatement order would be as follow:-

(i)   property not gifted under the deceased's will;

(ii) the residuary estate;

(iii) general money gifts from an unspecified source (such as a bank account); and

(iv) specific object gifts (such as jewelry, cars, etc).

While the beneficiaries of the deceased's estate are generally not responsible for the payment of debts left by the deceased, they do in a roundabout way end up paying for at least some of these debts. This is because assets which would otherwise have gone to them will be taken from the estate and sold in order to pay off the deceased's debts. This has the effect of reducing the value of the estate that is left to the beneficiaries (particularly the residuary beneficiaries). Some beneficiaries could, depending on the level of debt owed by the deceased's estate, potentially be left with very little or nothing at all.

Priority of Payments in Insolvent Estates

If there are not enough assets to cover the payment of the deceased's debts, the estate is said to be insolvent. In the case of an insolvent estate, each state has laws which govern how the assets of the estate should be distributed and, in particular, the order in which creditors are entitled to be paid from the estate's assets.

While the order of priority varies from state to state, a representative order of priority can be seen from the Uniform Probate Code. The code sets out the order as follows:-

(i)   costs and expenses of administration;

(ii) reasonable funeral expenses;

(iii) debts and taxes with preference under federal law;

(iv) reasonable and necessary medical and hospital expenses of the last illness of the deceased, including compensation for persons attending the deceased;

(v)   debts and taxes with preference under state law; and

(vi) all other claims.

If an estate is insolvent, the beneficiaries will normally (see below) end up getting nothing even if the deceased had gifted specific property or specified sums of money to them under his will. Beneficiaries can only receive assets in probate if there are enough assets left over after all legitimate debts have been paid.

Remember to check the laws of the state in which the probate is being administered to determine the precise payment priority in that state as the priority can change from state to state.

What Assets Should Not Be Used to Pay Debts?

It's very important to remember that, as a general rule, it only the deceased's probate assets which should be used to discharge debts owed by the deceased's estate. While this general rule does not apply in the case of taxes; it nevertheless is of significance in relation to all other creditor claims.

Therefore, the proceeds of life insurance policies, pay-on-death accounts, assets owned jointly as well as assets held in a living trust need not (in many states) be used to pay debts of the estate. Furthermore, there is no obligation on the surviving family of the deceased to discharge any bills owing by the deceased from their own funds or from non-probate assets. The simple truth is that if there are not enough probate assets to pay all the creditors – some will just have to do without!

Finally, it's also important to note that under most state laws, the deceased's surviving spouse and minor children whom were being supported by the deceased at the time of his death are entitled to a reasonable allowance in money out of the estate for their maintenance during the period of administration. The family allowance is exempt from and has priority over all claims other than claims for homestead allowance. Therefore, it is possible that the family of the deceased can receive assets from an insolvent estate. For more on this, see chapter 11.

ESTATE TAX

Chapter Overview

In this chapter, we will look at some of the different types of taxes which may be payable following a person's death. It will be your responsibility as executor to ensure that these taxes are paid by the estate.

Chapter

10

CHAPTER 10

ESTATE TAX

Responsibilities for Payment of Tax

As the executor, administrator or personal representative of an estate, your duties will almost always include filing and paying taxes on behalf of the deceased and the estate. Alternatively, if you are a trustee of a living trust, tax liabilities that would have fallen to the estate may fall to be discharged by the trust following the deceased's death. However, where the deceased left both a living trust and probate has opened on the deceased's estate, you will not (in your capacity as trustee) generally be responsible for payment of taxes by the estate. This is because, for tax purposes, where the deceased was both the creator and trustee of a living trust that trust will be regarded as being transparent for tax purposes and will therefore still form part of the deceased's estate on death. In which case, an executor dealing with the administration of the deceased's estate should deal with the discharging of any estate tax liabilities and personal income tax liabilities. Where the probate estate is insufficient to pay the taxes, the executor may require the trustee of the living trust to contribute funds from the trust to help meet the estate tax liabilities of the estate or the income tax liabilities incurred by the deceased prior to his death. Income taxes incurred after the deceased's death will be paid separately by the executor of the probate estate and the trustee of the living trust depending on whether the asset that created the income was in the estate or the living trust.

For the purposes of this chapter, we will use the term executor to encompass the roles of personal representative and trustee.

Taxes are a priority expense, meaning that they must be paid before most other creditors and certainly before any of the assets are distributed to the heirs or devisees of the estate. (As a vocabulary reminder, heirs inherit when there is no will, devisees or beneficiaries are named in the will to inherit. For the purposes of this chapter, we use the term heirs regardless.)

The tax maze is a complicated one, with differing taxes, deadlines and taxing authorities all in the mix. That is why most executors consult with a tax professional to ensure that all tax responsibilities are fulfilled. A certified public accountant, enrolled agent, or tax attorney will be a valuable resource to avoid making costly mistakes. When looking to use a tax professional, ask that professional about his experience dealing with state and federal income and estate taxes for a deceased person's estate. Some tax professionals have ample experience with living individuals and businesses, but may lack sufficient knowledge to help you with the tax requirements of an estate.

In some instances, someone else may take on the responsibility for filing certain tax returns, but you will most likely have to coordinate with that person to ensure that they pay whatever portion of the tax is owed by the estate. Remember, as an executor, the responsibility to ensure the estate pays taxes rests with you – and not with anyone you allow or delegate to deal with the task. By way of simple example, if you are the executor of the deceased's estate but not the surviving spouse, the surviving spouse may file the deceased's last income tax returns as part of a joint filing. Yet, paying the deceased's share of the income tax will still be the responsibility of the estate and you will be responsible to see that the estate pays it.

Note that the last sentence of the previous paragraph does not say that you must pay the taxes from your personal assets! In most situations, the executor is not required to discharge the deceased's personal taxes or indeed the estate's taxes from the executor's own funds. The money used to discharge these taxes will come from the estate – whether directly from cash held in the estate or from the proceeds of sale of the deceased's assets. In some cases, the estate may not have enough funds to pay the taxes, such as where most of the assets were held in a living trust. In those situations, the trustee and the executor (if they are different) are required to cooperate to see that the taxes are paid. The taxing authorities do not look kindly on not receiving their money, so even if there is no estate opened because everything passed outside probate, the taxing authorities expect that the person or entities that received the deceased's assets, whether through an estate, trust, or beneficiary designation, will be responsible for paying the taxes if the estate itself doesn't have enough assets to do so.

WARNING: If you, as the executor, make a payment to either a creditor or heir and then find that the estate doesn't have enough to pay the taxes you may become personally liable for payment of any outstanding taxes. This is because a presumption is raised that you failed in your duty as executor to ensure that the estate's assets are paid out in accordance with the manner and priority required by law and you must therefore bear the penalty for this – unless of course you can get the creditor or heir to give the assets back to the estate and you subsequently use them to discharge any outstanding taxes. That's why it's very important not to distribute assets to creditors or heirs until the tax liabilities are clearly determined and then only if you are very confident that distributing assets will still leave enough funds in the estate to pay the taxes.

This chapter will first address income taxes of the deceased and then income taxes of the estate. Later in the chapter, you will also read about estate, death and inheritance taxes that might be owed.

Income Taxes

Federal Income Taxes of the Deceased

As an executor, you are responsible for filing all tax returns that would have been required of the deceased were he alive. If the deceased had filed all his tax returns in a timely manner prior to his death, you will at a minimum have to determine if a tax return is required for the year in which the deceased died and the previous year. For example, if the deceased died in November and had filed and paid his taxes for the previous calendar year and all previous years, you will only be responsible for any filings required for the year in which the deceased died. However, if the deceased died in March, it is quite possible that returns had not yet been filed for the previous calendar year. In such circumstances, you will be responsible for any filings due both for the previous year and the year in which the deceased died.

Things get more complicated if the deceased failed to file required tax returns for any of the years before he died. You would also be required to file those in your job as executor. As a result, it is a good idea for you to check the deceased's records for at least the last three years to see if tax returns were filed. If you cannot tell from the deceased's records whether returns were filed, you may contact the Internal Revenue Service and request a transcript of the deceased's tax returns that the IRS has on file. You can request a transcript from the IRS by telephone on 1-800-829-1040, or order one by mail using IRS form 4506T (Request for Transcript of Tax Return). This form and many others are available on the IRS website at www.irs.gov.

Keep in mind that there may be no federal income tax returns required if the deceased did not have sufficient gross income. If the deceased owed any other tax, such as Medicare tax or alternative minimum tax, you will have to file a tax return regardless of the deceased's level of income. If the deceased is owed a tax refund, you will want to file a return regardless of whether it is otherwise required. To claim a refund on behalf of the deceased, you may need an extra form, IRS Form 1310 (statement of Person Claiming Refund Due a Deceased Taxpayer). Even if you determine that a federal income tax return is not required, you may decide to file an IRS form 56 (Notice Concerning Fiduciary Relationship). This form lets the IRS know that you are responsible for the estate's tax issues and you should receive any tax notices for the deceased or the estate.

The following Filing Requirement Table describes the income thresholds that require filing of a federal income tax return. The income requirements are based on the deceased's filing status, the deceased's age on December 31st of the tax year and the maximum gross income the deceased can have earned before a return is required. These numbers are current as of tax year 2014 reflecting updates where applicable, Keep in mind that some income does not count towards this maximum, such as tax-exempt social security income. If the deceased was retired, his or her income may have mainly been from social security. As a result, the deceased may not have filed income taxes before he died and one may not be required after his death. For more on what constitutes gross income, read the instructions to IRS Form 1040.

Filing Requirement Table (Information obtained from www.irs.gov. 2014)

Deceased Filing Status	Age	Max. Income
Single	Under 65	$10,000
Single	65 or older	$11,500
Head of Household	Under 65	$12,850
Head of Household	65 or older	$14,350
Married, filing separately	Any Age	$3,900
Married, filing jointly	Both spouses under 65	$20,000
Married, filing jointly	One spouse 65 or older	$21,200
Married, filing jointly	Both spouses over 65	$22,400
Qualifying widow(er)	Under 65	$16,100
Qualifying widow(er)	65 or older	$17,300

If you determine that a tax return is required, you will need to file IRS form 1040 and any of the schedules or attachments that the Form 1040 and its instructions indicate are applicable. The Form 1040 is due on April 15th (or if the 15th falls on a Saturday or Sunday, the next business day) of the year after the end of the applicable tax year. So, if the deceased died in November, the return is due on the following April 15th. If the deceased died in March, the return for the year he died is due in about 13 months, which is April 15th of the following year. Filing extensions are allowed for up to six months, but any taxes due must be paid by April 15th even if there is an extension to file the return. See IRS form 4868 for the grounds and methods to file for an extension.

When you file the return, you will use the deceased's social security number as the tax identification number. You need to write the word "DECEASED," the deceased's name and the date of death across the top of the tax return. If filing a joint return, you should write the names and addresses of the deceased and the surviving spouse in the spaces for the names and addresses on the front of the return. If you are not filing jointly, write the deceased's name in the first space for a name on the front of the return and the personal representative's name and address in the second space (where spouse would have gone if the return was filed jointly). You will need to attach a copy of the letters of authority or other court document that appointed you as executor of the deceased's estate. The instructions that come with the IRS Form 1040 include the appropriate address to which you should mail the return based on where the deceased lived at the time of his death.

The tables that follow indicate the tax rates effective for 2013/2014 that are applicable to individual taxpayers based on filing status. These tables have been extracted from information provided by the

Internal Revenue Service at www.irs.gov.

Filing Single			
Taxable Income:		Tax:	
Over	But not over	+%	On amount over
$	$		$
0	9,075	10%	0
9,075	36,900	15%	9,075
36,900	89,350	25%	36,900
89,350	186,350	28%	89,350
186,350	405,100	33%	186,350
405,100	406,750	35%	405,100
406,750	-----	39.6%	406,750

Filing Jointly or Surviving Spouse of Deceased Who Died In Tax Year			
Taxable Income:		Tax:	
Over	But not over	+%	On amount over
$	$		$
0	18,150	10%	0
18,150	73,800	15%	18,150
73,800	148,850	25%	73,800
148,850	226,850	28%	148,850
226,850	405,100	33%	226,850
405,100	457,600	35%	405,100
457,600	-----	39.6%	457,600

Married Filing Separate			
Taxable income:		Tax:	
Over	But not over	+%	On amount over
$	$		$
0	9,075	10%	0
9,075	36,900	15%	9,075
36,900	74,425	25%	36,900
74,425	113,425	28%	74,425
113,425	202,500	33%	113,425

Married Filing Separate			
Taxable income:		Tax:	
202,500	228,800	35%	202,500
228,800	-----	39.6%	228,800

Head Of Household			
Taxable income:		Tax:	
Over	But not over	+%	On amount over
$	$	.	$
0	12,950	10%	0
12,950	49,400	15%	12,950
49,400	127,550	25%	49,400
127,550	206,600	28%	127,550
206,600	405,100	33%	206,600
405,100	432,200	35%	405,100
432,200	----	39.6%	432,200

State and Local Income Taxes of the Deceased

Depending on where the deceased lived and worked, you may also be responsible for filing a state income tax return in addition to the federal return. Some states charge income tax on income earned in that state even for non-residents, so if the deceased earned income from a job or business located in another state, it is important to check that state's filing requirements for non-residents. Some localities, such as counties and cities, may also require income tax.

The requirements for local counties and cities are too varied for inclusion in this chapter, but can often be determined by contacting the tax collector or treasurer of the county or city.

Some states do not have an individual income tax and thus no return would be required. These states include Alaska, Florida, Nevada, New Hampshire, South Dakota, Texas, Washington and Wyoming. When an income tax return is required, it is usually due the same day as the federal income tax return (usually April 15th), but sometimes the state requirement may vary by a few days if the federal deadline fell on a weekend or holiday.

The table that follows provides information on the tax rates and standard deductions/exemptions applicable in each state. This table is created from information provided by the Federation of Tax Administrators at www.taxadmin. org.

State Income Tax Rates for Individuals				
For 2014 Tax Year				
Does Not Include Local Income Taxes				
State	Marginal Rates and Tax Brackets Filing Single	Standard Deduction Married	Personal Exemptions Single	Dependents
Alabama	2% > $0	$3,000	$1,500	$300
	4% > $500			
	5% > $3K			
Alaska	No Income Tax			
Arizona	2.59% >$0	$4,200	$2,100	$2,300
	2.88% > $10K			
	3.36% > $25K			
	4.24% > $50K			
	4.54% > $150K			
Arkansas	1% > $0	$46 (C)	$23 (C)	$23 (C)

State	Marginal Rates and Tax Brackets Filing Single	Standard Deduction Married	Personal Exemptions Single	Dependents
	2.5% > $3,700			
	3.5% > $7,400			
	4.5% > $11,100			
	6% > $18,600			
	7% > $31,000			
California	1% > $7455	$208(C)	$104 (C)	$321 (C)
	2% > $17,676			
	4% > $27,897			
	6% > $38,726			
	8% > $48,942			
	9.3% > $250,000			
	10.3% > $300,000			
	11.3% > $500,000			
	12.3% > 1,000,000			
	13.3% > --------			
Colorado		$7,800	$3,900	$3,900
Connecticut	3.0% > $0		Varies	$0
	5.0% > $10,000			
	5.5% > $50,000			
	6.0% > $100,000			
	6.5% > $200,000			
	6.7% > $250,000			
Delaware	2.2% > $2,000	$210 (C)	$110 (C)	$110 (C)
	3.9% > $5,000			
	4.8% > $10,000			
	5.2% > $20,000			
	5.55% > $25,000			
	6.75% > $60,000			
Dist. Columbia	4% > $0	$3,350	$1,675	$1,675
	6% > $10,000			
	8.5% > $40,000			
Florida	No Income Tax			

State	Marginal Rates and Tax Brackets Filing Single	Standard Deduction Married	Personal Exemptions	
			Single	Dependents
Georgia	1% > $0	$5,400	$2,700	$3,000
	2% > $750			
	3% > $2,250			
	4% > $3,750			
	5% > $5,250			
	6% > $7,000			
Hawaii	1.4% > $0	$2,080	$1,040	$1,040
	3.2% > $2,400			
	5.5% > $4,800			
	6.4% > $9,600			
	6.8% > $14,400			
	7.2% > $19,200			
	7.6% > $24,000			
	7.9% > $36,000			
	8.25% > $48,000			
	9.00% > $150,000			
	10.00% > $175,000			
	11.00 > $200,000			
Idaho *	1.6% > $0	$7,800	$3,900	$3,900
	3.6% > $1,380			
	4.1% > $2,760			
	5.1% > $4,140			
	6.1% > $5,520			
	7.1% > $6,900			
	7.4% > $10,350			
Illinois	3% of modified income reported on federal return	$4,000 (C)	$2,000(C)	$2000(C)
Indiana		$2,000	$1,000	$1,500
Iowa	0.36% > $0	$80	$40	$40
	0.72% > $1,494			

State	Marginal Rates and Tax Brackets Filing Single	Standard Deduction Married	Personal Exemptions Single	Dependents
	2.43% > $2,988			
	4.5% > $5,976			
	6.12% > $13,446			
	6.48% > $22,410			
	6.8% > $29,880			
	7.92% > $44,820			
	8.98% > $67,230			
Kansas	3.5% > $0	$4,500	$2,250	$2,250
	4.9% > $15,000			
Kentucky	2% > $0	$40 (C)	$20 (C)	$ 20 (C)
	3% > $3,000			
	4% > $4,000			
	5% > $5,000			
	5.8% > $8,000			
	6% > $75,000			
Louisiana	2% > $0	$9,000	$4,500	$1,000
	4% > $12,500			
	6% > $50,000			
Maine	2% > $0	$7,800	$3,900	$3,900
	6.5% > $5,200			
	7.95% > $20,900			
Maryland	2% > $0	$6,400	$3,900	$3,900
	3% > $1,000			
	4% > $2,000			
	4.75% > $3,000			
	5% > $100,000			
	5.25% > $125,000			
	5.5% > $150,000			
	5.75% > $250,000			
Massachusetts	5.25%	$8,800	$4,400	$1,000
Michigan	4.25%	$7,526	$3,763	$3,763

State	Marginal Rates and Tax Brackets Filing Single	Standard Deduction Married	Personal Exemptions Single	Dependents
Minnesota *	5.35% > $0	$7,300	$3,650	$3,650
	7.05% > $24,270			
	7.85% >$79,730			
Mississippi	3% > $0	$12,000	$6,000	$1,500
	4% > $5,000			
	5% > $10,000			
Missouri	1.5% > $0	$4,200	$2,100	$1,200
	2% > $1,000			
	2.5% > $2,000			
	3% > $3,000			
	3.5% > $4,000			
	4% > $5,000			
	4.5% > $6,000			
	5% > $7,000			
	5.5% > $8,000			
	6% > $9,000			
Montana	1% > $0	$4,480	$2,240	$2,240
	2% > $2,800			
	3% > $4,900			
	4% > $7,400			
	5% > $10,100			
	6% > $13,000			
	6.9% > $16,700			
Nebraska	2.46% > $0	$252 (C)	$126 (C)	$126 (C)
	3.51% > $2,240			
	5.01% > $17,500			
	6.84% > $27,000			
Nevada	No Income Tax			
New Hampshiare	5% > $0	$2,400	None	None
New Jersey	1.4% > $0	$2,000	$1,000	$1,500

State	Marginal Rates and Tax Brackets Filing Single	Standard Deduction Married	Personal Exemptions	
			Single	Dependents
	1.75% > $20,000			
	3.5% > $35,000			
	5.525% > $40,000			
	6.37% > $75,000			
	8.97% > $500,000			
New Mexico *	1.7% > $0	$7,800	$3,900	$3,900
	3.2% > $5,500			
	4.7% > $11,000			
	4.9% > $16,000			
New York	4% > $0			$1,000
	4.5% > $8,000			
	5.25% > $11,300			
	5.9% > $13,350			
	6.45% > $20,550			
	6.65% > $71,150			
	6.85% > $205,850			
	8.82 % > $1,029,250			
North Carolina*	6% > $0	$2,300	$1,150	$1,150
	7% > $12,750			
	7.75% > $60,000			
North Dakota *	1.51% > $0	$7,800	$3,900	$3,900
	2.82% > $36,250			
	3.13% > $87,850			
	3.63% > $183,250			
	3.99% > $398,350			
Ohio	0.59%> $0	$3,300	$1,650	$1,650
	1.17% > $5,200			
	2.35% > $10,400			
	2.94% > $15,650			
	3.52% > $20,920			
	4.11% > $41,700			
	4.70% > $83,350			

State	Marginal Rates and Tax Brackets Filing Single	Standard Deduction Married	Personal Exemptions Single	Dependents
	5.45% > $104,250			
	5.92% > $208,500			
Oklahoma	0.5% > $0	$2,000	$1,000	$1,000
	1% > $1,000			
	2% > $2,500			
	3% > $3,750			
	4% > $4,900			
	5% > $7,200			
	5.25% > $8,700			
Oregon	5% > $0	$376 (C)	$188 (C)	$1 (C)
	7% > $3,150			
	9% > $7,950			
Pennsylvania	3.07% > $0	None	None	None
Rhode Island *	3.75% > $0	$7,500	$350	$3,750
	4.75% > $58,600			
	5.99%> $133,250			
South Carolina *	0% > $0	$7,800	$3,900	$3,900
	3% > $2,850			
	4% > $5,700			
	5% > $8,550			
	6% > $11,400			
	7% > $14,250			
South Dakota	No Income Tax			
Tennessee	6% > $0 (interest and dividend income only)	$2,500	$1,250	
Texas	No Income Tax			
Utah	5% > $0	None (Credit Instead)	Varies	Varies
Vermont *	3.55% > $0	$7,800	$390	$3,900
	6.8% > $36,250			

State	Marginal Rates and Tax Brackets Filing Single	Standard Deduction Married	Personal Exemptions Single	Dependents
	7.8% > $87,850			
	8.8% > $183,250			
	8.95% > $398,350			
Virginia	2% > $0	$1,860	$930	$930
	3% > $3,000			
	5% > $5,000			
	5.75% > $17,000			
Washington	No Income Tax			
West Virginia	3% > $0	$4,000	$2,000	$2,000
	4% > $10,000			
	4.5% > $25,000			
	6% > $40,000			
	6.5% > $60,000			
Wisconsin	4.60% > $0	$1,400	$700	$700
	6.15% > $10,750			
	6.50% > $21,490			
	6.75% > $161,180			
	7.75% > $236,600			
Wyoming	No Income Tax			

* - These states allow personal exemption or standard deductions as provided in the IRC

Federal Income Taxes of the Estate

After a death, while the deceased may not be earning income any longer, his assets may still be producing income. That income is generally paid to the estate (or the living trust if the assets were in the trust). For example, if the deceased owned stocks or other investments, any appreciation or depreciation in those investments that occurred after the date of death but before distribution to the heirs might be a taxable income or a deductible loss to the estate. Therefore, as a general rule, the estate will need to file an income tax return if it has assets that earn income or incur losses. Of course, as executor the responsibility for making this filing will fall to you.

In order to file an income tax return, the estate must have a tax identification number. The deceased's social security number is not a valid tax identification number for income or losses that accrue after the death of the deceased. To obtain a tax identification number for the estate, you must file an IRS form SS-4 (Application for An Employer Identification Number), or you can obtain a tax identification number online at the IRS website, www.irs.gov. There is no deadline by which you must obtain a taxpayer identification number, but you will need one to open a bank account and file the tax returns for the estate.

Unlike with an individual's tax return, the estate can choose its tax year, meaning that it might choose a calendar year or a fiscal year. A fiscal year can be useful if the deceased died in the middle of the calendar year, especially if the estate is able to distribute all of its assets within twelve months from the date of death. Assume, for example, that the deceased died in May and his assets are distributed in April of the following year. If the estate is taxed on a calendar year, it will file one return for all of the income earned from May to December and a second return from January to April. If the estate chooses a fiscal year from May 1 to April 30, then it will only have to file one return. However, once the estate chooses its year by filing its first tax return, it cannot change to a different reporting period without getting approval from the IRS.

The estate may also choose its method of accounting, usually the cash method or the accrual method. Like the choice of accounting periods, once the estate makes its choice in its first return, it must continue to use that method for subsequent returns. If the estate's income in a taxable year is less than $600, the estate usually is not required to file an income tax return for that year. However, if the estate makes a distribution to a non-resident alien, that is, someone who is neither a resident nor a citizen of the United States, the estate must file an income tax return regardless of the amount of income.

When filing the income tax return, you will file IRS form 1041. If the estate chooses a calendar year reporting period, the Form 1041 is due by April 15th of the year following the end of the tax year. If the estate chooses a fiscal year reporting period, the form is due by the 15th day of the 4th month following the end of the reporting period. If we use our example above with a reporting period of May 1 to April 30, then the Form 1041 is due August 15th.

At the same time that you must file the IRS form 1041, you must provide an IRS form K-1 (Form 1041) to all heirs of the estate and file a copy of that K-1 with the IRS. The K-1 reports to the heir and the IRS how much of the estate's income was distributed to a particular heir. If the income was distributed to the heir, then the heir is responsible for reporting that income on his tax return and paying the appropriate tax on it. If the income was kept in the estate during the tax year, then the estate will pay the income tax. If an heir is a non-resident alien, you will also have to file his income tax return reporting the inheritance and paying the necessary tax. You use IRS Form 1040NR for that purpose.

The following table indicates the federal income tax rates applicable to trusts and estates from 2013. If you compare these rates to those applicable to individuals, you will see why it is often preferable to distribute income to the heirs and have the heirs pay tax on the income rather than keeping the income in the estate and having the estate pay the income.

Estates and Trusts Federal Income Tax Rates (This table is provided in the Instructions to IRS Form 1041)				
Taxable income:		**Tax:**		
Over	**But not over**	**Tax**	**+%**	**On amount over**
$	$	$		$
0	2,400	-	15	0
2,400	5,600	360.00	25	2,400
5,600	8,500	1,160.00	28	5,600
8,500	11,650	1,972.00	33	8,500
11,650	......	3,011.50	35	11,650

State and Local Income Taxes of the Estate

Depending on where the deceased lived and worked, you may also be responsible for filing a state income tax return for the estate. In some states, this will be called a Fiduciary Income Tax Return. As with individual income tax, some states charge income tax on income earned in that state even for non-residents, so if the estate earns income from an asset located in another state, it is important to check that state's filing requirements. Some localities, such as counties and cities, may also require income tax. Most of the states that do not have an individual income tax also do not tax the income of estates. When an estate or fiduciary income tax return is required, it is usually due on April 15th of the year following the reporting year.

Estate and Inheritance Taxes

Federal Estate Tax

The federal government requires an estate to file an estate tax return whenever the value of the estate, plus any taxable gifts that were made by the deceased during the deceased's lifetime, exceeds the applicable threshold. Legislation passed by the Senate on 31 December 2012 and by the House of Representatives a day later on 1 January 2013 has set that threshold at $5.25 million (which includes a provision for inflation). Any amount transferred in excess of $5.25 million will be taxable at the rate of 40%. A threshold of $5.34m has been announced for 2014.

If the deceased left his entire estate to his spouse, there will be no estate tax due regardless of the value of the estate. However, the law still requires an executor to file an estate tax return if the estate value exceeds the exclusion amount discussed above.

The estate tax return IRS form 706 (United States Estate (and Generation Skipping Transfer) Tax Return) is due within nine months of the date of the deceased's death. You can receive an automatic six month extension to file the estate tax return by filing IRS Form 4768 ((Application for Extension of Time To File a Return and/or Pay U.S. Estate (and Generation-Skipping Transfer) Taxes)). Even if you file for an extension to file the tax return, you must still pay the estimated taxes due by the nine month deadline.

The following table applies to estates where the deceased died after January 1 2013. The table is created from information provided in the instructions for IRS Form 706. Note that estate tax is only payable after the value of the gross estate has passed the $5.25M mark, which increases to $5.34 from January 1 2014.

UNIFIED RATE SCHEDULE					
Amount of Taxable Estate		**The Federal Estate Tax**			
(Column A) From	(Column B) To	Amount of Tax already paid on Column A	Tax Rate on amount in excess of Column A	Max Additional Tax in This Round	(Column E) Total tax
0	$10,000	0	18%	0	$1,800
$10,000	$20,000	$1,800	20%	$2,000	$3,800
$20,000	$40,000	$3,800	22%	$4,400	$8,200
$40,000	$60,000	$8,200	24%	$4,800	$13,000
$60,000	$80,000	$13,000	26%	$5,200	$18,200
$80,000	$100,000	$18,200	28%	$5,600	$23,800
$100,000	$150,000	$23,800	30%	$15,000	$38,800
$150,000	$250,000	$38,800	32%	$32,000	$70,800
$250,000	$500,000	$70,800	34%	$85,000	$155,800
$500,000	$750,000	$155,800	35%	$92,500	$248,300
$750,000	$1,000,000	$248,300	39%	$97,500	$345,800
$1,000,000	$1,250,000	$345,800	41%	$102,500	$448,300
$1,250,000	$1,5000,000	$448,300	43%	$107,500	$555,800
$1,500,000	$2,000,000	$555,800	45%	$225,000	$780,800
$2,000,000+	•	–	45%	•	•

State and Local Estate and Inheritance Taxes

Many states impose an estate or inheritance tax. A state estate tax operates like the federal estate tax and is imposed on the estate. A state inheritance tax is a tax paid by the heirs to the estate on the amount they received as an inheritance. While you are usually required to file the return whether the tax is an estate tax or an inheritance tax, the difference between the two types of taxes affects whether the tax is applied to the entire estate or proportionally among the heirs. Some local municipalities may also impose an estate or inheritance tax. For example, Nebraska does not have an estate or inheritance tax, but each county in Nebraska has an inheritance tax.

The filing deadlines for various state estate or inheritance taxes varies, but the most common deadline is the same as the deadline for filing the federal estate tax return, which is nine months from the date of death of the deceased. The following table describes the type of tax imposed and the exemption amount if the state has an estate tax. If a state is not listed in this table, it has neither an estate nor an inheritance tax.

State, Estate Or Inheritance Tax Table - This table is created from information provided by various sources, including the Tennessee Department of Revenue (www.tennesee.gov/revenue), The State Tax Roundup (www.bankrate.com) and CCH (www.finance.cch.com) and other websites.

STATE	TYPE OF TAX	EXEMPTION AMOUNT
Connecticut	Estate Tax	$2,000,000
Delaware	Estate Tax	$5,250,000
D. Columbia	Estate Tax	$1,000,000
Hawii	Estate Tax	$5,250,000
Indiana	Inheritance Tax	N/A
Illinois	Estate Tax	$4,000,000
Iwoa	Inheritance Tax	N/A
Kansas	Estate plus Inheritance	N/A

STATE	TYPE OF TAX	EXEMPTION AMOUNT
Kentucky	Inheritance Tax	N/A
Maine	Estate	$2,000,000
Maryland	Estate plus Inheritance	$1,000,000
Massachusetts	Estate	$1,000,000
Minnesota	Estate	$1,000,000
Nebraska	Inheritance (at county level)	N/A
New Jersey	Estate plus Inheritance	$675,000
New York	Estate	$1,000,000
North Carolina	Estate	N/A
Ohio	Estate	N/A
Oklahoma	Estate	N/A
Oregon	Estate	$1,000,000
Pennsylvania	Inheritance	N/A
Rhode Island	Estate	$910,725
Tennessee (separate inheritance tax)	Estate Plus Inheritance	$2,000,000
Vermont	Estate	$2,750,000
Washington	Estate	$2,000,000

Note: States will revise their taxes throughout each calendar year. As such, it is recommended that you verify the figures in this table before placing any reliance on them for estate tax or inheritance tax purposes.

DISTRIBUTING ASSETS AND CLOSING THE ESTATE

Chapter Overview

In this chapter, we look at the formalities associated with the distribution of the deceased's assets and the closing of his estate.

CHAPTER 11

DISTRIBUTING ASSETS AND CLOSING THE ESTATE

Closing the Estate and Distributing the Assets

Once all of the estate's assets have been collected and all of its debts and taxes paid, you will be able to distribute the surplus estate assets to the beneficiaries named in the deceased's will or to the 'heir-at-law' entitled to receive those assets on intestacy. However, before you make those final distributions, there some procedural matters that you will need to attend to.

Depending on the type of probate and the laws of the state in which that probate is taking place, you will need to:

- prepare an 'accounting' for the probate court setting out details of the financial transactions that took place during the administration of the deceased's estate;

- prepare and submit a plan to the probate court setting out how you plan on distributing the assets of the deceased's estate, and petition the court to approve that plan; and

- prepare and submit a statement indicating that all federal and state taxes owing by the estate have been discharged.

In addition, if you are seeking compensation for carrying out your services as executor, you may also need to file a petition seeking payment. That petition will be filed in conjunction with the petition to approve the final distribution plan for the estate.

Assuming that the accounting is in order, and the court grants an order approving your distribution plan, you will be free to proceed with distributing the assets of the estate. Once you have completed those distributions, the estate can be closed and you will be discharged from any further duties and responsibilities as executor.

What is an Accounting?

An accounting is a document that sets out details of the incomes and expenditures of an estate over a particular period of time. It will generally contain the following pieces of information:-

- the accounting period covered by the accounting;

- details of the initial inventory of estate assets and the value of each asset;

- details of all income and assets received during the accounting period;

- details of all disbursements made during the accounting period;

- details of all assets currently in the executor's possession;

- a reconciliation explaining the movement of any cash balances during the accounting period; and

- any other relevant information that the court might need to know about. For example, details of any claims due, contingent expenses, advancements, investments, disposal of assets, loss of assets, etc.

In certain states, a copy of the estate's bank account statement for the financial period covered by the accounting will need to be appended to the accounting document, as will copies of receipts and vouchers evidencing the expenditures referred to in the accounting. Vouchers are receipts which are signed by recipients when receiving payments from the estate.

You should check the laws of the state in which the probate is taking place to determine what precisely needs to be included in the accounting. If you are in any doubt as to what to include, seek the assistance of the local court clerk, an attorney and/or an accountant.

Sample Form

Sample Waiver of Account by Distributee - State of California

Name, Address and Telephone Number of Person Without Attorney:

_____

In Pro Per

SUPERIOR COURT OF THE STATE OF CALIFORNIA

COUNTY OF SANTA CLARA

In the Matter of the Estate of   ) Case No.:

)

)

) WAIVER OF ACCOUNT BY

DISTRIBUTEE

)

    Deceased.   )

)

_____)

[Name] _____ [being the
sole distributee/ one of the distributees] of the estate of [name]
_____, the deceased herein, does hereby
waive the filing and settlement of a final account by [name]
_____ as personal representative.

Dated: _____   _____

_____   (Signature)

_____

(Type or print name)

The Requirement for an Accounting

There are two specific types of accountings that may be required over the course of administering an estate. The first type is an interim accounting, while the second type is a final accounting.

An interim accounting will need to be prepared and filed with the probate court at the end of each year during the administration of the estate until the estate actually closes. Given the work and cost involved in preparing and filing an accounting, it is important that you don't unnecessarily allow the administration to carry on for any longer than necessary. If you do, the costs to the estate will mount up. A final accounting, on the other hand, only needs to be filed when you are in a position to carry out a final distribution of the estate's assets – i.e. after the payment of all taxes and creditors' claims.

Once an accounting has been prepared, you may need to submit it to the probate court for review. If the probate court is satisfied with the accuracy and content of the report, it will take no further actions save that, in the case of a final accounting, it will approve the distribution of the estate's assets as per the distribution plan. If, on the other hand, the court raises any queries in relation to the accounting, you will need to provide the relevant explanations and supporting documents to the court.

To avoid a situation where the court raises queries in relation to the accounting, it is usually helpful to engage the services of an accountant to assist you in the preparation of the accounting(s).

Waiving the Requirement for an Accounting

While, more often than not, an accounting will be required, the laws in many states allow for the requirement to be waived in certain circumstances. For example, if the beneficiaries named in the deceased's will provide written confirmation confirming that (i) they waive their entitlement to receive an accounting or (ii) that they have received their respective shares of the deceased's estate, the requirement to provide an accounting to the court (and the beneficiaries) can be dispensed with.

In closing the estate, the letter of waiver or confirmation will need to be provided to the probate court instead of the accounting. In order for the court to accept it, the letter must be signed by every beneficiary entitled to receive under the deceased's will, and not just some of them.

A sample form waiving the requirement for an accounting is set out on the next page. In order to obtain the correct form for use in the state in which probate is taking place, you should contact the relevant probate court.

Sample Form

Sample Accounting - State of Colorado	
☐ District Court ☐ Denver Probate Court _____County, Colorado Court Address: IN THE MATTER OF THE ESTATE OF: ☐ Deceased ☐ Protected Person Attorney or Party Without Attorney (Name and Address): Phone Number: E-mail: FAX Number: Atty. Reg.#: ☐ INTERIM ☐ FINAL ACCOUNTING FOR PERIOD:	COURT USE ONLY Case Number: Division: courtroom:

The undersigned states: That the following is a true and complete account of the administration of this estate during the period shown, both dates inclusive.

_____

Signature and Title of Fiduciary

_____

_____

_____

_____

Type or print name, address & tele.# of Fiduciary

NOTE: See Rule 31 of the Colorado Rules of Probate Procedure for filing requirements and instructions.

SUMMARY OF CASH RECEIPTS AND EXPENDITURES ONLY

Cash Balance on hand at beginning
of period of this accounting $_____

Total cash received or collected
during period of this accounting $_____

Total cash paid out during period
of this accounting $_____

Cash Balance on hand at end of period
of this accounting $_____

REMARKS AND NONCASH TRANSACTIONS

CASH RECEIVED OR COLLECTED DURING PERIOD

Date   From Whom and for What: Amount
_____   _____   _____
_____   _____   _____

                    Total Cash received or collected   _____

CASH PAID OUT DURING PERIOD

Date   From Whom and for What: Amount
_____   _____   _____
_____   _____   _____

                    Total Cash paid out   _____

_____

ASSETS REMAINING AT END OF PERIOD

Even where a letter of waiver or confirmation is filed with the probate court, you will probably still need to file a report setting out details of any compensation requested by you for carrying out the role of executor, as well as for any fees payable to the estate's attorney (if any).

Formulating a Plan for the Distribution of the Estate Assets

In addition to preparing an accounting (assuming one is required in the state in which the probate is taking place), you will also need to formulate a plan detailing how you intend to distribute the estate's assets. While this plan will largely be determined by the terms of the deceased's will (assuming that the deceased died testate), there are a number of things which can have an impact, in some cases significant, on the manner in which the estate assets can be distributed. These include:-

- ademption;

- the doctrine of lapse;

- simultaneous death;

- a spouse's right of election;

- disinheriting a child;

- homestead allowance;

- family allowance for support;

- the exemption for the benefit of the family;

- right to remain in the family home;

- right to receive family residence;

- right to automobiles;

- right to reimbursement of funeral bill;

- abatement of assets; and

- disclaimed inheritances.

We consider each of these items further below.

Ademption

"Ademption" is a legal term used to describe the situation where a gift of a particular piece of property (such as a motor vehicle, a piece of jewelry, an antique, etc) under a will fails because the object in question is no longer in the deceased's estate at the time of his death. Where this happens, the gift is said to have been "adeemed".

By way of a simple illustration, if the deceased left his black Jaguar Roadster to his favorite nephew under the terms of his will, but before his death sold the car, the gift to the nephew would fail. In the circumstances, the deceased's nephew is not normally entitled to receive a different gift (whether in the form of cash or otherwise) in substitution for the gift described in the deceased's will.

However, states that have adopted the Uniform Probate Code have attempted to abolish or scale back this common law doctrine of ademption by awarding beneficiaries certain rights where property gifted to them under a will has been disposed of by the deceased before his death. For example, under the code, a beneficiary would be entitled to the following in lieu of the failed gift:-

(i) the balance of any purchase monies owing to the deceased at the time of his death by the purchaser of the gifted property;

(ii) the proceeds of insurance monies payable in respect of the gifted property where that property has been destroyed or stolen;

(iii) the balance of any monies payable to the estate where the gifted property was acquired as a result of foreclosure, or obtained in lieu of foreclosure;

(iv) any real property or tangible personal property owned by the testator at death which the testator acquired as a replacement for specifically devised real property or tangible personal property; and

(v) in certain cases, a cash gift equal in value to the gifted property provided that the gifted amount would not be inconsistent with the testator's overall plan regarding the distribution of his estate.

It's important that you take special note of the provisions of paragraph (iv) above as they refer to one of the most common ademption scenarios encountered by executors when probating an estate. By way of illustration of the principle, let's suppose that the deceased gifted his 1954 Jaguar Roadster to his nephew under the terms of his will. After having made his will, the deceased sold that car and bought a Mercedes Benz. The deceased later replaced the Mercedes Benz with an Aston Martin and, at the time of his death, owned the Aston Martin. Under the rule in paragraph (iv), the deceased's nephew would be entitled to receive the Aston Martin in substitution for the Jaguar Roadster because it's a direct replacement item for the gifted property. If, however, the deceased had bought stock in a mutual fund with the proceeds of sale from the Jaguar or Mercedes, the nephew would not be entitled to the stock as it is not a direct replacement for the car – the replacement must be on a like-for-like basis.

Interestingly, it's also worth noting that where a beneficiary is gifted the proceeds of a particular bank account, and the funds in that account are transferred to another account before the deceased's death, the beneficiary can still be entitled to those funds on the basis of the 'like-for-like' exchange described above.

A bequest may also be adeemed if the deceased gave the gifted property to the intended beneficiary during his lifetime rather than waiting for the gift to be made following his death. This type of ademption is referred to as "ademption by satisfaction" as the gift to the beneficiary was satisfied prior to the gift in the deceased's will taking effect.

A gift of money or cash under a will cannot generally be adeemed. If there is insufficient funds in the deceased's estate to pay the cash gift to the beneficiary, you may need to sell some of the estate's assets (usually the assets in the residuary estate) in order to raise the necessary funds.

The Doctrine of Lapse

In the normal course, if a beneficiary named in a will dies before the testator, the gift made to that beneficiary will 'lapse' and become part of the testator's residuary estate – unless of course an alternate beneficiary is named to receive that gift. Where the gift becomes part of the residuary estate, the residuary beneficiaries (i.e. those beneficiaries entitled to the residuary estate) will ultimately receive that gift. This process by which a gift lapses and becomes part of the residuary estate is commonly referred to as the 'doctrine of lapse'.

If a residuary beneficiary dies before the testator the position changes a little in that, unless an alternate residuary beneficiary is named in the testator's will, a partial intestacy will be deemed to have occurred. As a result, that part of the residuary estate gifted to the deceased beneficiary will pass by intestate succession to the deceased's heirs-at-law - as if the testator made no will in relation to that part of his estate. In the absence of the testator's will expressly providing for it, the other residuary beneficiaries (if any) will not normally be entitled to take the deceased beneficiary's share of the estate as part of their overall entitlement to the residuary estate. This rule is known as the "no residue of a residue" rule.

Historically, this rule caused a considerable amount of difficulty for the families of deceased beneficiaries who often ultimately ended up receiving nothing from the testator's estate notwithstanding that they had, indirectly through the deceased beneficiary, stood to benefit from that estate. Fortunately, in more recent times, legislators in a number of states (including many that have adopted the Uniform Probate Code) have sought to address that hardship by introducing certain anti-lapse rules. These rules save the gift where it has been made to certain beneficiaries - usually members of the testator's family who themselves have children. Where the anti-lapse rules apply, the children of the deceased beneficiary will inherit whatever the deceased beneficiary was entitled to receive under the testator's will.

A testator can, however, override these anti-lapse rules by stating in his will (i) that the gift in question will only go to the beneficiary named in his will if that beneficiary survives him or (ii) that the anti-lapse rules shall not apply in relation to gifts made under his will. Where these types of provisions are included, the status quo outlined above will continue to apply and gifts will lapse in the usual way.

In determining whether a beneficiary survived the testator or not, the laws in a number of states provide that the beneficiary must survive the testator for a minimum period of time before he can be legally determined to have survived the testator. For example, the Uniform Probate Code provides that in order for a beneficiary to survive the testator, he must survive him by at least 120 hours. If the beneficiary dies before the full 120 hours have expired, he will be legally deemed to have pre-deceased the testator.

The Uniform Probate Code also regulates the inheritance rights of the residuary beneficiaries where one of them dies. In particular, section 2-604(b) of the Code provides that "...if the residue is devised to two or more persons, the share of a residuary devisee that fails for any reason passes to the other residuary devisee, or to other residuary devisees in proportion to the interest of each in the remaining part of the residue". This means that if two or more people are entitled to receive the residuary estate, and one dies, then the remaining residuary beneficiaries will be entitled to receive the deceased beneficiary's share of the residue estate in the same percentages that they were entitled as amongst themselves to receive the remainder of the estate. Where this rule applies, it therefore overrides the 'no residue of a residue' rule referred to above.

Simultaneous Death

The simultaneous death of a testator and a beneficiary can cause significant problems and confusion when probating an estate. It occurs where two people die in circumstances which make it unclear as to which one survived the other. From a probate perspective, this is of significant importance given that the right of a beneficiary to receive a gift is often premised on the requirement that the beneficiary survives the testator. In some cases, the required survival period is set out under the testator's will or under state law. In other cases, both the testator's will and the laws of the state in which the probate is taking place are silent on the issue.

In practice, however, most wills and trusts contain survivorship clauses which require the beneficiary to survive the testator or trust maker (i.e. the 'settlor') in order to be entitled to receive a gift under that instrument. These types of requirements can be helpful where both parties die within a short period of time as they serve to reduce the administration costs and taxes associated with the administration of the same set of assets in two different estates.

In determining the question of who died first, the court will look at all of the circumstances surrounding the deaths before reaching a determination. Where the evidence presented to the court is insufficient to allow the presiding judge to make a precise determination, that judge will usually have the right to draw a conclusion based on the facts to hand unless state law provides otherwise. To assist judges in making their determinations, many states have enacted the Uniform Simultaneous Death Act or similar laws of their own.

In the case of the Uniform Simultaneous Death Act, and while it has been adopted in varying forms in different states, it generally provides that where two people die within 120 hours of each other or in circumstances where it is not possible to determine who died first, property will be inherited and distributed as if each person had predeceased the other. These provisions have the effect of preventing property from passing into the estate of a person who is already deceased - the consequence of which would be that the property would need to be distributed immediately from that second estate to a beneficiary of the deceased person.

 Did You Know?

The following states have adopted the Uniform Simultaneous Death Act:- Alaska, Arizona, Arkansas, Colorado, District of Columbia, Hawaii, Kansas, Kentucky, Montana, New Hampshire, New Mexico, North Carolina, North Dakota, Ohio, Oregon, South Dakota, Utah, Virginia and Wisconsin.

The provisions of the Simultaneous Death Act will not of course apply where evidence is available to prove that one person survived the other or where the testator's will contains its own survivorship clause which overrides the provisions of the act.

By way of illustration, consider the case of Mark and Alison, a married couple with no children. They die in a car accident in circumstances where it cannot be ascertained who died first. Neither of them had executed a will so both of their families claim their assets. In the circumstances, the courts look to the Uniform Simultaneous Death Act to help resolve the dispute. Under the provisions of the act, Mark is deemed to have predeceased Alison, but Alison is also deemed to have predeceased Mark. Their respective assets are divided equally among their heirs-at-law in accordance with the rules of intestacy. The same result would apply if Alison died 100 hours after Mark as she failed to survive Mark by the required 120 hours under the act. However, if Alison died 140 hours after Mark, matters would change substantially as Alison's estate will be entitled to claim the share of Mark's estate that Alison would have been entitled to had she not died.

As an executor, if the testator and a beneficiary die in close proximity to each other, you will need to carefully check the rules regarding survivorship in both the deceased's will and under the laws of the state in which the probate is being carried out to determine the inheritance rights of the parties. If you are in any doubt as to the position, speak to a licensed attorney.

A Spouse's Right of Election

The laws of many states allow a surviving spouse the right to choose between (i) what he or she has been left under the terms of their deceased spouse's will and (ii) a specific defined share of his or her deceased spouse's estate. This share, which is set out under state law, is commonly referred to as a spouse's "minimum" or "elective" share. While the exact amount of this share varies from state to state, the general rule of thumb is that:

- if the deceased spouse had no children, the surviving spouse is entitled to half of the deceased spouse's net estate; or

- if the deceased spouse had children, the surviving spouse is entitled to one third of the deceased spouse's net estate. However, some states do impose minimum financial entitlements. For example, under New York law, a surviving spouse is entitled to the greater of $50,000 or one third of the deceased spouse's net estate.

Important Note

In this section, for convenience and illustrative purposes, we refer to a female spouse's elective right. In practice, however, a male spouse also has exactly the same rights.

If a deceased spouse leaves more than the elective share of his net estate to his surviving spouse, his spouse would not ordinarily exercise her right of election (i.e. the right to accept a lesser amount in this case) unless she felt that it would be more advantageous (for tax reasons or otherwise) to allow a greater part of the deceased spouse's estate to pass to some of the other beneficiaries named in the deceased's will.

In reality, the surviving spouse's right of election is only valuable where the deceased spouse leaves her less than the elective share of his net estate. By way of illustration, consider the following example. A husband and wife live in New York. The husband dies and, under the terms of his will, leaves $100 to his wife and the remainder of his entire estate to his children. Under New York law, the wife has the right to accept the gift made to her under her husband's will (i.e. $100) or claim her elective share (i.e. the greater of $50,000 or one third of her husband's net estate) notwithstanding the terms of her husband's will. If the wife makes the election, she will receive the relevant amount from her husband's estate. The balance of the husband's estate will pass to his children as stipulated in his will. However, in paying the elective share, the executors of the husband's estate may need to sell some of the estate's assets in order to raise funds to make the payment. Where assets are sold, the sale can of course impact the rights of other beneficiaries under the will (if any) particularly where gifted assets are sold to raise the funds. In which case, ademption (see above) and abatement (see below) can apply.

Important Note

Divorce usually terminates the right of a surviving spouse to claim a share of his or her deceased spouse's estate.

If a surviving spouse decides to take her elective share rather than take what was left to her under the terms of her deceased husband's will, then she will forfeit the right to receive any gifts made to her under that will. That said, in many cases where the election is made, the surviving spouse will often be allowed to take some or all of the items (depending on what was gifted to the surviving spouse) left to her under her husband's will. This is particularly so in circumstances where the amount left to her under her husband's will is in fact less than her elective share entitlement. The balance of any amount owing to the surviving spouse after she has taken the specific gifts left to her under her husband's will (or those of them that she wants) is usually then satisfied in cash rather than via the transfer of other specific items of property to her.

In states that have adopted the Uniform Probate Code, certain assets which passed to the surviving spouse during the life of her deceased spouse or on his death (including assets that passed to her by means of survivorship) will be deemed to have been transferred to her in part satisfaction of her elective share. As a result, only the balance of her share will need to be transferred to her from the deceased's probate estate. The rules in this regard do however vary from state to state, so you will need to check the laws of the state in which the probate is being conducted to determine the precise rules that apply.

Where a surviving spouse elects to take her elective share instead of any gifts made to her under her deceased spouse's will, as executor, you will need to construe the deceased spouse's will as if the additional property taken by the surviving spouse had in fact been disposed of before the deceased's death. As a result, the rules of abatement set out above will apply to the interpretation of that will and the distribution of the assets under it.

Important Note

The decision by a surviving spouse to take his or her elective share should generally be in writing and should be signed and acknowledged by the surviving spouse. Where the surviving spouse is legally incompetent, the election should be signed by the surviving spouse's guardian or conservator. Once signed, a copy of the election should be filed with the probate court clerk. Thereafter, the clerk will usually send a copy of the written election to the executor.

While the law varies from state to state, a spouse who wishes to claim her elective share can do so in writing or by appearing before the probate court and making an appropriate application for her elective share. In some cases, the right can be exercised by taking no action at all.

However, irrespective of the manner in which an election is made by the surviving spouse, as executor you will need to ensure that the election is made within the time frames set out under state law. These time frames tend to be between one and six months from the date on which the executor is first appointed to office. Furthermore, in many states, executors are required to notify the surviving spouse of his or her legal right to claim an elective share. This notification is usually required to be made on a specific probate form which contains a relatively detailed summary of the elective share entitlement. If the surviving spouse fails to make the election within the required time frame, she will lose that right and will have to make do with whatever has been left to her under her deceased husband's will.

As you will have gathered from the foregoing, in most states, a deceased spouse cannot easily disinherit his spouse. This is also the case in community property states where a surviving spouse is generally entitled to half of the couple's community property irrespective of the terms of the deceased spouse's will. If you are in any doubt as to the rights of a surviving spouse in the deceased's state of residence, we recommend that you consult an attorney.

Important Note

If a spouse wishes to claim an elective share, he must do so in writing within a specific time frame.

Whatever choice the surviving spouse makes, it's important to remember that she will (unless the terms of her deceased husband's will provides otherwise) still be entitled to avail of any other legal rights that she may have by virtue of being a surviving spouse. Depending on state laws, these rights might include the right to buy certain estate assets from the deceased spouse's estate, to remain in the family home for a specific period of time (usually a year), to claim and receive an allowance for her support, to receive automobiles and watercraft owned by her deceased husband and to avail of such other rights as a surviving spouse would ordinarily be entitled to under law.

Disinheriting a Child

Unlike the position regarding spouses, it is possible for a testator to completely disinherit his children in virtually every state in the U.S. Only in Louisiana is this right restricted. A testator can disinherit his children if his will (i) expressly states that the testator intended to disinherit his child and/or (ii) makes only a nominal gift to that child (such as a gift of $10). If the testator's will fails to mention any of his children in one of these two manners, it would be open for that child to challenge the terms of the will on the basis that the testator simply forgot to include the child in the will. On that basis, the child could obtain a large portion of the testator's estate. In some cases, that amount may be equal to what the child would have received had the testator died intestate.

More importantly, in some states, the laws relating to the disinheritance of children apply equally to grandchildren. That means that where a grandparent fails to mention a grandchild in his will, that grandchild could potentially challenge the will of his grandparent if he was not expressly mentioned in the will. As such, in order for a grandparent to successfully disinherit a grandchild, he would also need to ensure that the grandchild is expressly disinherited in the same way as set out above in relation to children.

In certain states, children are entitled to claim a share of a deceased parent's property regardless of the terms of their parent's will. For example, if the deceased parent lived in the state of Florida and was the head of their family for tax purposes, they would be prohibited from leaving their home to anyone besides their spouse or children. If the deceased parent purported to do so under his will, both his spouse and his children could bring a legal challenge to quash the gift and direct that the property be transferred to them.

The laws relating to the disinheritance of children do vary from state to state and can be complex. If you are dealing with an estate in which there is an attempt to disinherit a spouse or a child, you should seek the advice of an attorney. Remember, the legal costs will be borne by the estate and not you personally.

Homestead Allowance

In all states, a surviving spouse is entitled to receive a payment from her deceased spouse's estate known as a 'homestead allowance'. The amount of this allowance varies from state to state and is often dependent on the value of the deceased's estate. Under the Uniform Probate Code, it is suggested that adopting states provide an allowance of $15,000 to the surviving spouse. However, the code leaves it to the discretion of those states to determine the level of the allowance provided in those states. If the deceased person did not have a spouse at the time of his death but had minor or dependent children, those children shall be entitled to receive the full level of the homestead allowance in equal shares.

The payment of the homestead allowance from the deceased's estate has priority over the payment of all claims against the estate and, as such, is paid even before the creditors of the estate. In addition, it's also payable in addition to any share of the deceased's estate passing to his surviving spouse or his dependent children (i) under his will (unless the will provides otherwise of course), (ii) under the rules of intestacy or (ii) following the exercise by the surviving spouse of her right to claim her elective share.

Important Note

If a spouse or dependent child wishes to claim their homestead allowance or the family allowance (see below), he or she may be required under state law to make that claim in writing and within a specific period of time following the deceased's death. In addition, some states impose a requirement that, in order to claim the homestead or family allowance, the claimant must survive the deceased spouse or parent by a specific number of days.

If you are in any doubt as to the laws relating to homestead or family allowance in the state in which you are conducting probate, you should contact your attorney or the probate court clerk for more information.

Family Allowance for Support

In addition to their entitlement to a homestead allowance, surviving spouses and dependent children are also entitled to claim an allowance in money from the deceased's estate in order to provide for their maintenance during the administration of the deceased's estate. The amount of this allowance varies from state to state. The Uniform Probate Code, while leaving it to the discretion of adopting states to fix the amount of the allowance, suggests that it should be reasonable having regard to the previous standard of living and other financial resources available to the family members. In other states, the amount is limited. For example, state law in Ohio provides for a maximum allowance of $40,000. State laws also allow for the payment of the allowance as a single lump sum or in periodic installments.

You will need to check state law to determine the precise level of the allowance available in the state in which probate is taking place.

The Exemption for the Benefit of the Family

As well as the rights mentioned above, the laws in some states allow a surviving spouse to claim certain specific property owned by her deceased spouse at the time of his death. The surviving spouse can claim that property irrespective of whether the deceased spouse left that property to her under his will.

In some states that have adopted the Uniform Probate Code, for example, the property to which a surviving spouse is entitled to includes household furniture, automobiles, furnishings, appliances and personal effects not exceeding $10,000 in value. If the total aggregate value of such property in the deceased's estate is less than $10,000 the surviving spouse will be entitled to chose any other property of the deceased in order to make up the $10,000 total.

In determining the value of an item of property, the value of that property is deemed to be reduced by the amount any loans or similar obligations secured against it. So, for example, a car worth $20,000 that has a loan of $16,000 secured against it will only be deemed to be worth $4,000 for the purposes of determining whether it falls within the total $10,000 amount.

The right of a surviving spouse to claim this exemption takes precedence over the rights of creditors of the estate to receive payment. However, it is generally payable only after the homestead allowance and family allowance have first been paid. Again, like the other allowances, unless otherwise provided for in the deceased's will, this entitlement is in addition to the surviving spouse's entitlement under the deceased's will, on intestacy or upon claiming her elective share.

If the deceased spouse died leaving no living spouse, his children (if any) will be jointly entitled to receive this benefit.

 Important Note

If a surviving spouse or child wishes to claim this exemption, he or she may be required under state law to do so in writing within a specific time frame. In addition, depending on state law, he or she may need to survive the deceased spouse/parent by a specific number of days in order to claim this entitlement.

Right to Remain in the Family Home

Where a family home is gifted by the deceased spouse under the terms of his will, the surviving spouse may have a right under state law to remain in that house for specific period of time notwithstanding the gift. This period of time varies under state law and can range from a right to remain in the house for as little as a few months to life. If the family home is ultimately sold to raise funds to discharge debts of the deceased's estate, the surviving spouse may also be entitled to receive an amount from the estate equal to the fair rental value of the property.

Like the other entitlements of a surviving spouse described above, a surviving spouse will need to exercise her right to remain in the family home in writing and within a specific period. This period of time normally commences on the date of death of the deceased spouse or the date appointment of the executor (given that it's the executor on whom notice is generally served). If the right is not exercised within the required time frame set out under state law, it will lapse.

If, as executor, you receive any form of notice of election from a surviving spouse, you will need to carefully determine whether the form of notice is correct and, if so, whether it has been served within the correct time frames prescribed under state law. Again, the probate court clerk or an attorney should be able to assist you in making that determination.

Right to Receive Family Residence

Depending upon the value of a family home, the law in many states allows for a surviving spouse to receive that property as part of her entitlement to inherit from her deceased spouse's estate. Similarly, the laws in certain states give surviving spouses the right to purchase certain assets including the family home from her deceased spouse's estate where she does not have an entitlement to the asset outright. Any payment (which will be at fair market value) made by the surviving spouse for the asset will go directly to the deceased spouse's estate.

Similar to the exercise of other rights, notice must be served on the executor or, in some cases an application must be made to court to obtain its consent to purchase the asset in question. In each case, the surviving spouse will need to comply with the relevant time frames for making such elections and applications.

Right to Automobiles

In some states, the surviving spouse and/or children of the deceased spouse are entitled to have automobiles owned by the deceased at the time of his death transferred to them. Depending on the value of the automobile in question, this may be done outside of the probate process. Otherwise, an election must be made in the usual way as part of the probate process. The right may apply notwithstanding that the deceased spouse may have gifted those automobiles to a third party under his will. Written notice is again required and election time frames need to be complied with.

Right to Reimbursement of Funeral Bill

In some states, surviving spouses are entitled to be reimbursed by the deceased spouse's estate for the cost of any payments made by them in connection with the deceased's funeral.

Abatement of Assets

High levels of debt and a lack of liquid assets (such as cash) within the estate of a deceased person can create a situation where estate assets need to be sold in order to raise funds to pay those debts. This process of selling assets to pay debts is known as 'abatement'.

Where assets are sold to raise funds in this manner, it may result in a situation where the executor can no longer make all of the gifts stipulated under the deceased's will – as the assets will no longer be part of the deceased's estate when it comes to distributing the estate assets. If a situation arises where assets need to be abated in this manner, it can be advisable for an executor to call a meeting of the principal beneficiaries to advise them of the situation and of the assets that are to be sold. While there is no obligation to convene such a meeting, it can be beneficial to outline to the beneficiaries the consequences of the asset sales and why they are occurring.

The laws in many states set out an order of priority in which assets should be sold. In most cases, assets forming part of the residuary of the estate will be sold before assets that that have been specifically gifted.

Disclaimed Inheritances

Where a person is named as a beneficiary of a gift under a will, he is free to renounce or disclaim his right to receive that gift. Where he does so, the gift will pass to any alternate beneficiary named in the will to receive that gift. If no alternate beneficiary is named in the will, the gift will form part of the residuary estate and will ultimately pass to the beneficiary or beneficiaries entitled to receive the residue of the estate. A beneficiary who disclaims a gift cannot direct who should receive that gift in his stead.

A gift may be disclaimed for several reasons - because it's unwanted, carries heavy liabilities (property maintenance, for example), tax reasons, or because the intended beneficiary simply wants to pass the gift to the alternate beneficiary or residuary beneficiary.

If a beneficiary wishes to disclaim a gift made to him under a will, he should notify the executor of his decision as soon as possible as state law sets down specific time frames within which the gift can be disclaimed. For federal estate tax purposes, the beneficiary must sign a written disclaimer and file it within nine months of the testator's death. In each case, if you (as executor) receive any form of disclaimer from a beneficiary, you should check the laws of the probate state to determine whether it has been validly made.

Did You Know?

Your final job as executor will be to distribute the assets of the deceased's estate to the beneficiaries named in his will. Once you do this, you will normally be free to close the estate.

Petitioning the Court to Approve the Plan of Distribution

Once you have prepared your accounting and your proposed plan of distribution, the next step in the administration process will be to petition the probate court to convene a hearing for the purpose of approving the distribution plan – although a hearing will not be required in every state or in respect of every probate. Sometimes, the court will simply issue an order approving your plan without the need to have a hearing. You will need to check the precise requirements in the state in which the probate is being conducted.

Where a petition is filed, it will typically include the following parts:

- an accounting (unless you have received signed waivers from the interested persons waiving their right to an accounting);

- a report on the administration setting out a summary of the steps you took as executor in administering the estate;

- the distribution plan; and

- a petition requesting the court to approve the accounting (if filed), the distribution of the estate assets and any additional matters that require court approval such as, for example, the payment of fees to you as executor or to the estate's attorney.

Sample Form

Sample Petition for Final Settlement and Distribution
- State of Colorado

☐ District Court ☐ Denver Probate Court	COURT USE ONLY
_____County, Colorado Court Address: IN THE MATTER OF THE ESTATE OF: Deceased: Attorney or Party Without Attorney (Name and Address): Phone Number: E-mail: FAX Number: Atty. Reg. #:	Case Number: Division: Courtroom:

PETITION FOR FINAL SETTLEMENT AND DISTRIBUTION

1. Petitioner, as the personal representative of this estate, has collected and managed the assets, filed the inventory and accounting and performed all other acts required of petitioner by law.

2. The time for presenting claims which arose prior to the death of the deceased has expired.

3. The proposed schedule of distribution is attached.

4.   ☐ The court has previously determined testacy and heirs following lawful notice to all interested persons.

        ☐ The Registrar has previously informally admitted to

probate the deceased's will and petitioner affirms the
statements in the application for informal probate and
appointment of personal representative.

☐ Petitioner affirms the statements in the application for
informal appointment as personal representative of an
intestate estate.

5. ☐ Other:_____

_____

_____

PETITIONER REQUESTS that the court set a time and place of hearing; that
notice be given to all interested persons as provided by law; that after notice
and hearing, the court determine testacy and heirs if not previously determined;
determine the persons entitled to distribution; accept the final accounting
as presented; direct the personal representative to distribute the remaining
assets of the estate; and upon filing final receipts or evidence of distribution,
discharge the personal representative and any surety on the personal
representative's bond.

Date: _____

_____

Signature of attorney for petitioner   Signature of Petitioner

(Type or Print name, address, & tele. # below)

_____

_____

_____

Giving Notice of the Hearing

Where probate is taking place in a state that has adopted the Uniform Probate
Code, and indeed in various other states, you will be required to notify all
interested persons (including beneficiaries and heirs-at-law – see Chapter 8 for

a full list of interested persons) of the court hearing to approve the distribution plan.

In order to properly serve notice of the hearing on these people, you will need to complete an appropriate Notice of Hearing form (see sample form contained in the ensuing pages). Once completed, you will need to arrange to have a third party either mail or personally deliver the notice to each person who is entitled to receive notice of the hearing. You will generally not do this yourself as you will need to have a third party independently verify service of the notice by completing and signing a 'declaration of service' confirming that he or she has properly served notice on the interested parties. A sample declaration of service is included in the ensuing pages. However, the form of this declaration will vary from state to state.

The Notice of Hearing will need to be delivered to the interested parties within the time frame set out under state law. This timeframe normally requires that delivery be made at least 15 days before the hearing is due to take place. In most cases, the only document that you will need to send to the interested parties is the Notice of Hearing itself. However, you may wish to include a copy of the petition for settlement and distribution so that the recipients are clear on the proposed plan of distribution and the reasons why you are proposing to distribute the deceased's estate in that manner.

Finally, once the notice of the hearing has been served and the declaration of service has been completed, you will need to file the originals of both documents with the probate court clerk.

Sample Form

Sample Notice of hearing on petition for final settlement and distribution - State of Colorado	
□ District court □ Denver probate court _____County, Colorado court Address: IN THE MATTER OF THE Estate OF: Deceased: Attorney or Party Without Attorney (Name and Address): Phone Number: E-mail: FAX Number: Atty. Reg.#:	COURT USE ONLY Case Number: Division: Courtroom:
NOTICE OF HEARING ON PETITION FOR FINAL SETTLEMENT AND DISTRIBUTION	

TO ALL INTERESTED PERSONS:

A hearing on the Petition for Final Settlement and Distribution, a copy of which is attached to this Notice, will be held at the following time and location or at a later date to which the hearing may be continued.

Date and Time: _____

Courtroom or Division:_____

Address:_____

Interested persons have the responsibility to protect their own rights and interests within the time and in the manner provided by the Colorado Probate Code, including the appropriateness of claims paid, the compensation of personal representatives, attorneys and others and the distribution of estate assets. The court will not review or adjudicate these or other matters unless specifically requested to do so by an interested person. If any interested person desires to object, such person shall file specific written objections and shall furnish the personal representative with a copy at or before the hearing.

Attendance at this hearing is not mandatory. Actual distribution of estate assets normally does not occur at the hearing.

_____

Signature of Petitioner or Attorney for Petitioner   Date

_____

_____

_____

_____

Type or Print name, address & tele. # of Petitioner

NOTE: This form or CPC24-NA must be used in formal proceedings terminating an estate. (Section 15-12-1001 or 1002, C.R.S. and Rule 8.3, C.R.P.P.) Use of this form is limited to an appearance hearing.

CERTIFICATE OF SERVICE

I certify that on (date) _____, a copy of this Notice of Hearing on Petition for Final Settlement and Distribution was served on each of the following at the indicated address by:

☐ hand delivery   ☐ certified U.S. mail, postage pre-paid
☐ first class U.S. mail, postage pre-paid
☐ registered U.S. mail, postage pre-paid

Name and Address

_____

Signature of Person Certifying Service

NOTE: This certificate of service cannot be used in cases where personal service is required or used. Use CPC7-P (Personal Service Affidavit) or CPC8-A (Waiver of Service) for each person required to be served personally.

Distributing the Estate Assets

Once the hearing takes place, the court will usually allocate a period of time within which interested parties can raise objections to the accounting or the proposed plan of distribution. Assuming, however, that no objections are raised within that time period (usually 30 to 60 days depending on state law), you will be free to distribute the estate's assets in accordance with your plan of distribution. If an objection is raised, however, the probate court will consider the objection and make any changes to the distribution plan that it deems appropriate in the circumstances. It will also issue an order directing that you distribute the assets in the manner determined by the court.

Early Distributions

While the law varies from state to state, the general rule of good practice (and indeed the rule of law in many states) is that no assets should be paid out or transferred from the estate to the beneficiaries until all creditors' claims have been satisfied and all taxes have been paid. Of course, payment of some of the allowances and entitlements referred to earlier in this chapter (such as the homestead allowance) can be made. As such, it is possible to make some partial or early distributions from the estate before the final distribution is made. However, you should check state law carefully before making any such payments.

In order to transfer specific assets to the beneficiaries, you will need to evaluate the legal and procedural requirements applicable to the transfer of those assets. The ensuing pages of this chapter examine the transfer procedures associated with some of the more commonly held assets.

Transfer of Real Estate

Real estate is normally transferred to the beneficiary of the estate either by recording a deed, such as a personal representative's deed, or by recording details of the transfer on the court order approving the final settlement and distribution of the estate. State law will determine which of these procedures is appropriate. In either instance, you will need to file the appropriate document in the registry of deeds of the county in which the relevant property is located. Thereafter, the registry office will amend the register of titles to show the beneficiary as being the new owner of the property.

Transfer of Cars, Boats and Other Vehicles

In a number of states, one or more vehicles (in some cases up to a certain value only) can be transferred to the deceased's surviving spouse outside of the probate process. To effect the transfer, the surviving spouse will need to complete a declaration (known as an 'affidavit') setting out specific details in relation to the vehicle being transferred and presenting the completed declaration to the department of motor vehicles in the probate state. If the surviving spouse cannot avail of this non-probate transfer method or if the vehicle has been gifted by the deceased spouse to a different person under his will, you will need to complete a separate transfer document in the required state specific form in order to register the transfer of the vehicle. You may need to check with the department of motor vehicles in the probate state to determine the specific transfer requirements that apply. Be aware that, in some states, a tax can be levied when transferring vehicles from one person to another.

If the deceased gifted a boat under his will and that boat is registered with the Coast Guard (although very few are), you will need to check with them to determine what their specific transfer requirements are.

Transfer of Cash Accounts

Cash gifts, or pecuniary legacies as they are also called, can be made by simply writing a check drawn on the estate bank account in favor of the relevant beneficiary.

If you are planning on writing checks from the estate bank account, you should enquire from the bank as to whether it has any form of traceable checks that you can use. These are checks which, when cashed, will be canceled by the bank and returned to you. On the back of each such check, you can have the payee (i.e. the beneficiary) acknowledge receipt of the check in satisfaction of a gift made to him under the deceased's will. The payee can sign this acknowledgement when receiving the check from you. The cancelled and returned check will ultimately act as a voucher evidencing the beneficiary's receipt of his gift from the estate.

As not all banks provide traceable checks, you may simply wish to have the payee sign a standalone form of acknowledgement confirming that he has received the funds. Alternatively, instead of using a check, you could also transfer the funds by wire transfer to an account in the beneficiary's name or issue a bank draft to him. In each case, as the monies are extracted immediately from the estate's bank account, it has the added benefit of reducing the likelihood that you will have to wait weeks or even months for the beneficiary to cash a check before being able to close the account and the estate.

Transfer of United States Savings Bonds

You will need to contact the deceased's bank to obtain the appropriate form as well as details of the procedure involved in transferring the bonds to a beneficiary. Once the transfer is completed, the bonds will be re-issued in the name of the beneficiary. You will normally need to complete a Treasury Form PD 1455 and send the completed form back with a copy of your letters of authority, a copy of the deceased's death certificate and any certificate of title evidencing the bonds in order to instruct the bank to make the transfer.

Transfer of Broker Accounts

It's possible to transfer a broker account held with a brokerage firm or with a mutual fund company directly to a beneficiary. You will however need to contact the firm/company to determine whether they can simply change the name on the account or whether they will have to close the existing account and open a new one in the name of the beneficiary.

In dealing with the brokerage firm or mutual fund company, you will most likely need to send a copy of your letters of authority and a copy of the deceased's death certificate to them.

Transfer of Publicly Quoted Stocks and Bonds

To transfer stocks held by the deceased to a beneficiary, you will need to contact the company's share registrar (also called a transfer agent) and formally request that the stocks in question be transferred to and re-issued in the name of the beneficiary. If you are in possession of the stock certificate issued in the deceased's name, it should indicate the identity of the share registrar. If not, you can get the required details by contacting the company directly. Most quoted companies have a department that deals exclusively with shareholder and investor queries.

Once you determine who the registrar is, you will usually need to send the following documents to them (but call and check what documents they need before you send anything) in order to have the stock re-issued in the name of the beneficiary:-

- the original stock certificate relating to the quoted company in question;

- a letter of instruction from you, which is signature guaranteed by a bank, trust company or a brokerage firm registered with the New York Stock Exchange;

- a stock power of attorney, which again is signature guaranteed in the manner described above;

- a copy of your letters of authority; and

- a copy of the deceased's death certificate.

As you will need certain documents 'signature guaranteed' you may simply wish to have your broker deal with the transfer on behalf of the estate. There will invariably be a fee to pay, but it might be the quickest way for you to deal with matters. You will also have the choice of instructing the broker to open an account in the name of the beneficiary or to have the stocks in question re-issued 'in street name' in their brokerage account – as street accounts are easy to deal with. The choice, however, will be yours.

Did You Know?

What does "in street name" mean?

Where the securities and assets of a customer of a brokerage firm are held under the name of the brokerage firm, rather than the name of the customer who purchased those securities and assets, they are said to be held in 'street name'.

If you need to transfer municipal or corporate bonds from the deceased's estate to a beneficiary, you can do so in much the same way as outlined above for quoted stock. However, when it comes to 'bearer bonds' you should be aware that the proceeds payable in respect of same will be paid to the person who physically holds such bonds. There will be no formal transfer or registration procedure.

Transfer of Other Property

If you need to transfer any other property from the estate to a beneficiary, you can usually do so by signing a simple deed of assignment – which will normally need to be countersigned by the beneficiary. That said, if the transfer of a specific asset (such as real property, vehicles or stocks, for example) require you to use a specific form of transfer document, you will usually need to use that document in order for the transfer to be effective.

If you are in any way uncertain as to how you transfer legal title in a specific asset or as to what document you need to use to do so, you should contact an attorney for assistance.

Transfer of Joint Tenancy, Community and Other Survivorship Property

As the transfer of joint tenancy, community property and other survivorship property takes place outside of the probate process, you will not ordinarily have authority or responsibility as executor to deal with these matters. However, in practice, executors may often be surviving spouses or may have been joint owners of property with the deceased. As such, it's useful to touch on the topic in passing at least – particularly in the context of real property.

When it comes to dealing with real estate, the procedure for registering the transfer of the deceased joint owner's share to the other joint owners is fairly similar in all states. In most cases, the surviving owners will need to file a document with the land registry indicating that the deceased owner has passed away and that, as a result, they are now the sole owners of the jointly held property. Of course, if there is only one surviving owner, the property will be transferred into his or her name only.

In some states, the transfer can be completed by simply filing a copy of the deceased owner's death certificate in the land registry. Upon filing, the land registry will record the change in ownership of the property on the relevant title registers. In other states, however, the surviving joint owners need to sign a sworn affidavit confirming that they are the surviving joint owners and formally request that the title to the property be transferred into their sole names.

The procedure is generally straight forward. However, if you need to deal with the transfer of jointly held property, you may wish to check with the local land registry to determine the precise requirements that apply.

Distributing Property to Children

Depending on laws of the state in question, minors resident in a state are generally only entitled to have a nominal amount of property transferred in to their own names following the making of gifts to them under the terms of a will or on intestacy. This amount varies between approximately $1,000 and $5,000 depending on the state in question.

If a minor is gifted more than the permitted statutory amount under the terms of a will or on intestacy, it will not be possible for that minor to receive the gift directly. Instead, it will have to be given to a legal guardian, conservator, or trustee of the minor to manage on his behalf. This trustee or guardian will normally be named in the deceased's will. If not, the court will appoint someone to serve as the child's 'property guardian' and that person will hold and manage the property on behalf of the minor.

A court will often appoint the surviving parent as guardian, but this is not always the case. A third party or court appointed guardian could be appointed to deal with the property and, in such cases, that property guardian will have complete control over the minor's inheritance.

Obtaining and Filing Receipts

In advance of you being discharged from your office as executor, you will need to demonstrate to the probate court that the estate's assets have been distributed to the rightful beneficiaries. In order to do this, you will need to provide written receipts, signed by the beneficiaries, to the court. As such, it's important that you obtain a signed receipt from each person to whom you transfer estate property to. In certain circumstances, it may even be sensible to hold back on transferring a gift to a particular beneficiary unless he simultaneously signs an appropriate receipt acknowledging receipt of that gift. A sample form of a receipt is set out on the next page; and it should be required from each beneficiary.

However, you should be aware that many states now have prescribed forms of receipts which must be completed by the beneficiary and produced to the court. As such, you will need to check the laws in the state in which the probate is being administered to determine whether a prescribed form needs to be used or whether you can use a generic form. Each signed receipt will need to be filed with the probate court prior to filing a petition for your final discharge.

Sample Form

Sample Receipt and Release - State of California	
☐ District Court ☐ Denver Probate Court _____ County, Colorado Court Address: ☐ In the Interests of: ☐ In the Matter of the Estate of: Attorney or Party Without Attorney (Name and Address): Phone Number: E-mail: FAX Number: Atty. Reg. #:	**COURT USE ONLY** Case Number: Division: Courtroom:
RECEIPT AND RELEASE	

Received from _____,

☐ Personal Representative

☐ Conservator

☐ Partial

☐ Full payment and satisfaction of the following:

      ☐ the devise to me in the will under article(s) _____

      _____.

      ☐ my _____ share of the estate in the will under article(s)

      _____.

      ☐ my _____ share of the estate as heir.

      ☐ my distribution from the conservatorship case.

☐ Cash in the amount of $ _____.

☐ Tangible personal property described as: * _____

_____

The following securities: * _____

_____

_____

☐ Other (describe): * _____

_____

_____

☐ I grant a partial release and satisfaction to the fiduciary of the
   estate as to the above partial distribution.

☐ I grant a full and final release and satisfaction to the estate
   and to the fiduciary and his or her successors for any liability in
   connection with my interest in the estate.

Date: _____

Signature: _____

           (Type or print name below)

* Attach additional sheets as necessary.

Closing the Estate

Once you are satisfied that you have accounted for and distributed the
deceased's estate in full, you will be able to petition the court to have you
formally discharged from the office of executor. In most cases, this is done
informally by filing a statement with the probate court confirming that you have
done everything required of you as executor and requesting that the estate be
closed. At the same time as filing this application for an informal closing, you
will also need to send a copy of the application to all interested persons. If any

of the interested persons object to the closing of the estate, they may seek a formal hearing in court in order to address any outstanding issues or concerns that they may have. On the other hand, if no objections are filed within the time frame set out in the notice, the estate can be closed and your obligations as executor will usually end one year from date of the filing.

Depending on the law of the state in which the probate is being conducted, a particular period of time may need to have elapsed following the opening of the estate before you can file for an informal closing in the above manner. For example, the laws in states that have adopted the Uniform Probate Code generally require that a period of six months has elapsed before you can close the estate. In states that have not adopted the code, the period does vary.

Sample Form

Sample Statement for Informal Closing - State of Colorado	
☐ District court ☐ Denver probate court _____ County, Colorado Court Address: IN THE MATTER OF THE ESTATE OF: Deceased Attorney or Party Without Attorney (Name and Address): Phone Number: E-mail: FAX Number: Atty. Reg. #:	**COURT USE ONLY** Case Number: Division: Courtroom:
VERIFIED STATEMENT OF PERSONAL REPRESENTATIVE CLOSING ADMINISTRATION	

The undersigned personal representative of this estate states:

1. Six months have passed since the original appointment of a general

personal representative for this estate or at least one year has passed
since the deceased's death. The date of the original appointment was

_____.

2. Except as may be disclosed on an attached explanation, the undersigned or a
preceding personal representative has fully administered this estate by making
payment, settlement or other disposition of: all lawful claims; expenses of
administration; federal and state estate taxes, inheritance taxes and other death
taxes; and the deceased's estate's federal and state income taxes. The assets of
the estate have been distributed to the persons entitled to receive such assets in
the amount and in the manner to which they were entitled. If any claims are
listed on an attached explanation as remaining undischarged, an explanation of
arrangements for their disposition is also listed.

3. The undersigned has sent a copy of this statement to all distributees of this
estate and to all creditors or other claimants whose claims are neither paid
nor barred and has furnished a full account in writing of the undersigned's
administration to the distributees whose interests are affected.

4. No court order prohibits the informal closing of this estate. Administration
of this estate is not supervised.

This statement is filed for the purpose of closing this estate. The appointment
of the personal representative will terminate one year after this statement
is filed with the court if no proceedings involving the undersigned are then
pending. (§ 15-12-1003, C.R.S.)

As the personal representative and being sworn, I verify that the facts set forth
in this statement are true to the best of my knowledge, information and belief.
DATE:_____

_____

Signature of Personal Representative
(Type or Print name, address & telephone # below)

_____

_____

state of _____

County of_____

Subscribed and sworn to before me by the personal
representative on : _____

My commission expires _____

Notary Public/(Deputy) Clerk of court

CERTIFICATE OF SERVICE

I certify that on (date) _____, a copy of this
Verified statement of Personal Representative Closing

Administration was served on each of the following at the indicated address by:

☐ hand delivery   ☐ certified U.S. mail, postage pre-paid

☐ first class U.S. mail, postage pre-paid ☐ registered U.S. mail, postage pre-paid

Name and Address

_____

_____

_____

_____

Signature of Person Certifying Service

NOTE: This certificate of service cannot be used in cases where personal
service is required or used. Use CPC7-P (Personal Service Affidavit) or
CPC8-A (Waiver of Service) for each person required to be served personally

As an alternative to an informal closing of the estate, you can formally close the estate by convening a final hearing at which you will petition the court to expedite the termination of your duties as executor. In most states, you can do this at any time provided of course that the applicable period within which creditors can file claims against the estate has lapsed. Again, notice of the hearing must be provided to all interested persons.

At the hearing itself, if the judge accepts that you have properly administered the office of executor and have done everything that you ought to have done as executor, then an order of court will be issued closing the estate and determining your duties on such date as falls 30 days (usually) after the date of the order. This 30 day time frame is the time given to interested persons to appeal the judge's order. Of course, given the cost of making such appeals, it is seldom used unless potential litigation makes it useful or necessary.

Once the probate has closed and your role as executor has come to an end, you will cease to have authority to deal with estate assets. As such, if assets are discovered at any time after you have been discharged, the beneficiaries will need to petition the court to re-open the estate. This petition will also provide for the appointment of an executor to the re-opened estate. The person nominated as executor in the petition may or may not be you. Each state has specific forms and procedures applicable to the re-opening of an estate so do check the precise requirements with the local probate court should it become necessary.

Task Checklist

Are You Ready to Close the Probate Estate?

- Have you published a formal Notice to Creditors and allowed the relevant time for creditors' claims to lapse?

- Have you received any valid Creditor's Claims? If so have they been agreed and paid?

- Have you discharged all relevant taxes?

- If you are seeking remuneration for your services as executor, have you determined the amount of that fee?

- If you engaged attorneys, appraisers or accountants on behalf of the estate, have you determined and agreed the fees paid or payable to them?

- If you have completed ALL of the above, you may be ready to distribute the estate assets and close the estate.

What If the Estate isn't Ready to Be Closed?

Generally, executors are expected to file a petition for final distribution or a verified report on the status of the estate within one year after they have been officially appointed as executor. This one year period can increase to 18 months where a federal estate tax return is required to be made. The status report should indicate the condition of the estate, the specific reasons why it cannot be closed and distributed (e.g. ongoing litigation, tax audits, assets need to be sold, etc) and also the estimated time needed to close the estate.

A hearing will be convened in order to receive and consider the status report. Again, all interested persons have an entitlement to receive notice of the hearing. At the hearing itself, the court will consider the reasons for the delay in closing and will make any order it feels appropriate to expedite the closing.

If an executor fails to file a status report, any interested person may petition the court to have the executor file the report. More importantly, for you, if this occurs the court may reduce the level of compensation payable to you as executor of the estate or even terminate your appointment as executor.

CHAPTER 12:

THE SETTLING OF TRUSTS

Chapter Overview

While the task of settling a living trust is very similar to that of probating an estate, it's useful to touch on this area specifically as many executors often find themselves acting as both executor of somebody's estate and successor trustee of their living trust. So, in this chapter, we take a quick look at living trusts and the main tasks involved in winding them up.

Chapter

12

CHAPTER 12

THE SETTLING OF TRUSTS

What is a Trust?

A trust can be described as a fiduciary arrangement whereby one or more persons become the legal owners of trust property which they hold for the use and benefit of somebody else.

Did You Know?

A trust is a legal device established by a person, usually under written agreement, for the purpose of holding and managing real or personal property on behalf of and for the benefit of another.

Every trust arrangement has a number of core components. These include:-

    (i)   the grantor (also called a settlor, donor or creator) - the person who sets up the trust;

    (ii)   the objective of the trust – why it has been set up;

    (iii)   the trust property – the property which has been placed into the trust;

    (iv)   the trustee – the person who will manage the trust property;

    (v)   the beneficiaries – the people entitled to receive the trust property; and

(vi)   the rules of the trust.

These 'core components' must be contained in every trust. Usually, the terms of the trust are set out in either a deed or a will. In the case of a deed or declaration, the trust is said to be created by a "grantor" or, in the case of a will, by a "testator".

Under the terms of a trust, a grantor 'settles' trust property on one or more trustees for the benefit of one or more beneficiaries. The trustee, in turn, assumes an obligation to preserve and protect the trust property and generally manage the trust's affairs on behalf of the beneficiaries.

The standard of care that a trustee must observe in carrying out his obligations is one of the highest known to the law. A trustee must always act for the benefit of and in the best interests of the beneficiaries of the trust and never for his own personal gain. The trustee must also exercise due care and diligence in the management of the trust property. The obligations of a trustee extend to ultimately vesting or transferring the trust property to the beneficiaries upon the happening of a future event (e.g. when they attain a specific age, complete college or satisfy whatever conditions are set out in the trust document).

A trustee will have the similar fiduciary duties as those outlined for executors in Chapter 2.

Trust property can be any form of property, including cash, real estate and every type of personal property. The trust deed (or the will) basically just says what the trustee can do, can't do and must do. It may also define who can be a beneficiary and who can't.

What Exactly are Living Trusts?

A living trust is a particular type of trust that is used for estate planning purposes. It is a written agreement created for the simple purpose of holding ownership of assets outside of the grantor's probatable estate during his lifetime, and then distributing those assets to named beneficiaries after his death. By holding ownership of the assets outside of the grantor's estate in this manner, the assets will fall outside of the probate net. As the assets will not therefore be tied up in probate following the grantor's death, they can be quickly distributed to the beneficiaries of the trust.

A revocable living trust is created by simply executing an agreement (or deed) pursuant to which a trustee agrees to hold and manage certain trust property on behalf of the grantor. One of the unique features of revocable living trusts however is that the same person will, in the majority of cases, act as both grantor and trustee. By also playing the role of trustee, the grantor can maintain control over and use of the assets he transfers to the trust.

As living trusts are ordinarily revocable, the grantor reserves the right to revoke or terminate the trust and resume personal ownership of the trust property at any time. In addition, the grantor also maintains the right, exercisable at his discretion, to add to or withdraw assets from the trust property, to change the terms of the trust and even to make it irrevocable at some time in the future.

After the grantor (or the grantor and his spouse in the case of a joint living trust) dies, a person known as a successor trustee (like an executor in many respects) will step in to manage the trust property and to distribute it to the beneficiaries named in the trust deed. One or more successor trustees are usually named in the trust deed.

In some cases, the distribution of the trust assets by the successor trustee can be done in only a few weeks given that it all takes place outside of probate and away from the supervision of the court. However, if there are creditors and taxes to be paid, the process may become just as drawn out as the probate process. The living trust will cease to exist when all of the trust property has been transferred to the named beneficiaries.

Parties to a Living Trust

While the parties to a living trust are pretty much the same as those which are party to a normal trust, it's worth having a quick look at them at this juncture so that you can familiarize yourself with them. The principal parties are as follows:-

Grantor/Settlor	This is the person who sets up the trust.
Trustee	This is the person who will manage the trust property. With revocable living trusts, the grantor usually acts as trustee.
Successor Trustee	The successor trustee is the person who will step in to manage the trust property when the grantor dies or if he becomes incapacitated and unable to manage the trust property. When the grantor dies, the successor trustee will distribute the assets in the trust in accordance with the terms of the living trust agreement/deed. He will not, however, have any power to amend the terms of the trust agreement/deed.
Beneficiaries	These are the people who are entitled to receive the benefit of the trust's assets upon the grantor's death.

The Successor Trustee

The successor trustee is, as mentioned, the person who assumes control of the trust after the grantor (as initial trustee) becomes incapacitated and/or dies. Once the successor trustee assumes control of the trust, he will be obliged to manage and deal with the trust assets in accordance with the terms of the trust agreement. In the case of the grantor's death, the successor trustee will also be responsible for transferring ownership of the trust assets to the beneficiaries named in the trust agreement. In the case of a shared or joint trust (where there is more than one grantor), the successor trustee will take over control of the trust only when both trustees are incapacitated or dead. The successor trustee will have no authority to act while any of the grantors remain alive or capable of managing the trust.

The trust agreement will identify the person or persons who will act as successor trustee(s) of the trust. In most cases, this is usually a relative or a family friend of the grantor or the executor of the grantor's estate.

Similar to the position with executors, it's important to note that even where a person is named as a successor trustee in a trust agreement, he is under no obligation to carry out the role and cannot be forced to do so. He is perfectly entitled to decline the nomination. If he does so, the alternate successor trustee named in the trust document will be asked to take on the role. If no alternate is named or if none of the named alternates are willing to serve as successor trustee, the beneficiaries of the trust will need to petition the local court to appoint someone to fulfill the role.

Even where a person takes on the role as successor trustee, he or she is usually free to resign the position at any stage. However, many trust agreements prohibit an acting successor trustee from fully resigning until replaced or relieved by a new successor trustee. This is to ensure that the trust is not left unmanaged at any time. That said, a successor trustee cannot be forced to act, so a court petition may be necessary if a new successor trustee is not forthcoming.

What Must the Successor Trustee Do When the Grantor Dies?

When the grantor dies, it will be the successor trustee's responsibility to assume control of the trust estate and administer it in accordance with the terms of the living trust agreement. In much the same way as the deceased's estate is administered for probate, the administration process for trusts involves the collection of assets, payment of debts and taxes and the distribution of assets to the ultimate beneficiaries of the living trust.

In the majority of cases, the beneficiaries under a living trust will be the grantor's spouse and/or children. Of course, the grantor is free to choose any beneficiaries he wishes. That said, spouses do of course have certain legal rights and entitlements (as outlined in the previous chapter), the grantor's freedom to dispose of the assets in the trust may be restricted.

In any event, let's take a brief look at what's generally involved when it comes to administering a living trust.

Obtain Certified Copies of the Death Certificate

Similar to the administration of an estate in probate, one of the successor trustee's first tasks following the death of the grantor will be to procure copies of the grantor's death certificate. This certificate, together with an affidavit of trust under which the successor trustee confirms his right to represent the living trust, will need to be presented to third parties in order to prove that the successor trustee is lawfully entitled to deal with the trust assets. In most cases, financial institutions such as banks and life insurance companies will require these documents before allowing the successor trustee to access any accounts or policies held in the trust's name.

A death certificate can generally be obtained from the state office of vital records or from the local department of health, but there are some variations from state to state. The successor trustee could also contact the grantor's general practitioner or funeral director, each of whom should be able to procure a copy of the death certificate for him.

Obtain a Tax Identification Number for the Trust

Next, the successor trustee will need to make an application to the IRS in order to obtain a tax identification number for the trust. The application can be made using IRS Form SS-4. See Chapter 6 for more on obtaining Tax Identification Numbers.

In the case of a shared living trust (where there is more than one grantor), an application may need to be made for a tax number for each of the two resulting trusts. With a shared or joint trust, the trust splits into two separate trusts known as resulting trusts – one for the benefit of the deceased spouse and one for benefit of the surviving spouse. This split occurs immediately upon the death of the first spouse and, upon its occurrence, the trust created for the benefit of the deceased spouse becomes irrevocable – it cannot be changed. As this trust has become irrevocable, it will be necessary to obtain a tax identification number for it. Whether or not the trust created for the benefit of the surviving spouse requires a new tax identification number will depend on the nature of the original shared trust. If the joint trust placed the surviving spouse's share into a revocable trust for the spouse, a tax number for the spouse's trust will not be required. However, if the deceased's trust created an irrevocable trust for the spouse, sometimes called a Marital Trust, a tax number may be required.

Notify Beneficiaries

When the grantor dies, the successor trustee is obliged to notify all the potential beneficiaries of the grantor's death and of their possible entitlements under the terms of the trust document. This obligation to notify beneficiaries can be contained within the terms of the trust document or set out under state law. For example, section 7-303 of the Probate Code provides that:

> "the trustee shall keep the beneficiaries of the trust reasonably informed of the trust and its administration. In addition:
>
> (a) Within 30 days after his acceptance of the trust, the trustee shall inform in writing the current beneficiaries............of the Court in which the trust is registered and of his name and address.
>
> (b) Upon reasonable request, the trustee shall provide the beneficiary with a copy of the terms of the trust which describe or affect his interest and with relevant information about the assets of the trust and the particulars relating to the administration.
>
> (c) Upon reasonable request, a beneficiary is entitled to a statement of the accounts of the trust annually and on termination of the trust or change of the trustee."

As can be seen from paragraph (c), the successor trustee is not obligated to deliver a set of trust accounts to a trust beneficiary unless that beneficiary has actually requested a copy. The lack of a formal obligation to deliver accounts here is intended to avoid extensive administration burdens on the successor trustee's part while at the same time provide the beneficiary with adequate protection and sources of information should he so require.

In most cases, where a beneficiary requests an accounting in respect of the trust, the successor trustee will send the beneficiary a copy of the annual tax returns for the trust together with a narrative explaining the movements of trust assets and funds.

Collection and Management of Trust Assets

Having obtained a death certificate and completed an affidavit of trust, the next task for the successor trustee will be to take possession of the trust's assets and to evaluate what debts, claims, taxes and other expenses may be payable by the trust. The successor trustee should work very closely with the executor of the grantor's estate in order to determine what assets have been transferred into the trust and what debts and taxes might be due.

The successor trustee should commence the process by reviewing the trust agreement and trust records in order to establish what assets have been transferred into the trust and what debts might exist. In this respect, the successor trustee should review the schedule of trust assets at the back of the trust agreement/deed (if there is such a schedule) and carefully review any title deeds and certificates which are located amongst the grantor's possessions. Title deeds tend to give a clear indication as to whether assets have been legally transferred to the trust or not.

The successor trustee should, working in conjunction with the executor (if an executor is appointed), carry out a full search for assets which may belong to the trust. This search will be done in pretty much the same way as outlined in previous chapters for executors. The successor trustee will need to review the deceased grantor's records, contact financial institutions, contact the grantor's advisors, and so on.

Once the successor trustee locates the trust assets he will need to secure them in the same way as an executor should. Securities (especially bearer bonds), title deeds, jewelry and other items of substantial value should be placed in a safe deposit box or in a safe. Trust assets, such as real estate and other valuable items, should also be adequately insured against risks such as fire, damage, theft, loss and liability, as appropriate. To do this, the successor trustee will need to contact any insurers of such assets to ensure that the death of the grantor has not caused the termination of any of the existing policies. If any of these policies have been terminated or where no policy was previously in existence to cover some or all of the trust assets, the successor trustee should organize appropriate cover.

Once the assets are secured, the successor trustee should obtain a valuation of those assets.

Claim Life Insurance Proceeds

The successor trustee should contact any insurance company with whom the grantor held a policy of life insurance. If the living trust was named as a designated beneficiary on any of those policies, the successor should make a claim for any insurance proceeds due to the trust. The insurance company will require copies of the death certificate and an affidavit of trust from the successor trustee before releasing the funds to him. In addition, it will also require the successor trustee to fill out a standard claim form.

Once the insurance claim has been processed, the funds can be paid out to the trust. The successor trustee should, however, ensure that the funds are paid to a federally insured trust account pending subsequent release to the beneficiaries of the trust estate.

Gain Access to Bank Accounts and Other Financial Accounts

Each financial institution which held an account for the trust should be notified of the death of the grantor so that it can commence the process of releasing the proceeds of the trust accounts to the successor trustee. Again, similar to insurance companies above, the financial institutions will require copies of the death certificate and an affidavit of trust from the successor trustee. Again, released funds should be placed in a federally insured trust account.

Identify Debts Owed By the Grantor

A detailed examination of the grantor's affairs will need to be carried out in order to determine what debts may be due and owing by the trust. In this respect, the successor trustee should again work closely with the executor of the grantor's estate to identify these debts.

In the ordinary course, and unless the trust agreement says otherwise, there is no obligation on the successor trustee to use any of the trust assets to discharge debts owing by the grantor personally (as opposed to debts owing by the trust which must be paid from the trust's assets). It will be the responsibility of the executor of the grantor's estate to discharge those debts from the grantor's probate estate. However, where no probate is opened, most state laws will require the deceased debts be paid from the assets in the living trust.

Management of the Trust Assets

Similar to the job of executor, the successor trustee will also need to reduce unnecessary expenses of the trust estate, deal with depreciating assets, manage real estate, manage investments, discharge debts, etc. He will also need to take appropriate actions to ensure that the value of the trust estate is maintained. In addition, the successor trustee may need to sell some or all of the trust assets to pay debts of the trust estate or to facilitate the proper distribution of the trust estate – particularly where the residuary trust estate is divided amongst several beneficiaries in percentages or fractions.

For a more detailed discussion on the management of assets, see Chapter 6.

Maintain Proper Accountings of Trust Assets

A successor trustee will be under a duty to prepare an annual accounting in respect of the trust assets, unless the beneficiaries waive their rights to this or the trust agreement provides otherwise. The accounting should display details of the assets held by the trust at the date of death of the grantor and their current market valuations. The accounting should also include details of any income received, any expenditure made and any assets added to or taken out of the trust estate over the relevant accounting period.

Like an executor, the successor trustee will need to keep meticulous records of all disbursements from the trust. To this end, it is usually advisable for the successor to use checks in order to disburse monies from the trust estate's accounts. In this way, there will be an audit trail of all transactions carried out by the successor trustee on behalf of the trust. Of course, wire transfers are equally effective and provide an equally clear audit trail.

In order to determine market valuations for some of the trust assets, the successor trustee may need to engage the services of professional valuation agents such as stockbrokers, realtors, etc. The preparation of these valuations are important for the purpose of determining what federal estate tax, if any, will be owing by the grantor. As the living trust will be treated as transparent for tax purposes, the successor trustee will need to work closely with the executor of the grantor's estate in order to procure a combined market valuation for all of the grantor's assets at the date of his death and to ensure that appropriate taxes are paid.

Preparing and Filing Tax Returns

The successor trustee and the executor of the grantor's estate will be collectively responsible for the payment of the various taxes set out below. Payment should first come from the probatable estate and then from the trust estate if the probatable assets are insufficient to discharge the relevant tax liabilities.

Federal Estate Tax

The extent of the grantor's estate both inside and outside the trust estate will need to be determined. To the extent that the value of that combined estate exceeds the applicable tax threshold, estate tax will become payable. For details of applicable rates, see Chapter 10.

It's the responsibility of both the successor trustee and the executor to determine if any estate tax is due by the grantor's combined estate and, if so, to make an appropriate tax return. The successor trustee and executor have a period of nine months from the date of the grantor's death to file the tax return and to discharge any estate taxes that are due. An extension of six months may be obtained in certain circumstances.

Income Taxes

A final income tax return will need to be made for the grantor for the year of his death. The return should be made on IRS Form 1040. Again, the payment of tax should be coordinated with the executor.

Trust Income Tax Returns

Following the death of the grantor, all income generated by the living trust will need to be returned separately to the IRS. The return for the trust will be made on IRS Form 1041 for each calendar year. It is the responsibility of the successor trustee to ensure that these returns are made.

Remember, as mentioned above, where the living trust is a shared trust which splits into two separate resulting trusts, there will need to be two separate tax returns. The deceased's spouse's trust will file an IRS Form 1041 under its own specific tax number. The trust created for the benefit of the surviving spouse will be made using the spouse's tax number on IRS Form 1040 unless the shared trust was an AB trust creating at least one irrevocable trust (usually called the Marital or Family Trust), in which cases, the surviving spouse's trust will need to file a Form 1041 under its own tax number.

State Taxes and Pick-Up Taxes

Finally, the successor trustee and executor will also need to arrange for any state taxes or pick-up taxes which may be due and owing by the combined estate to be discharged.

Transferring Property to Beneficiaries

Once all of the assets have been collected in and all debts and taxes paid or provided for, the successor trustee can distribute the remaining trust assets in accordance with the terms of the living trust. The assets will either be distributed in cash or in kind if the trust includes specific tangible assets.

Of course, in order to properly carry out the distribution, the beneficiaries will need to have the trust assets re-registered in their names by the successor trustee. The successor trustee will need to go through the process for transferring title in the trust assets over to the beneficiaries. After the re-registration is accomplished, the assets are deemed to have been effectively transferred to the beneficiaries of the trust. In each case, the successor trustee should have each beneficiary sign an acknowledgement to confirm that he has received the distribution in question.

Administering a Child's Trust

The duties of the successor trustee normally terminate once he has distributed the trust assets to the beneficiaries of the trust. However, where the grantor has created a sub-trust for any of his children or indeed any other minor beneficiary named in the living trust, the successor trustee will need to continue acting as trustee of the child's trust. In essence, the successor trustee will need to manage the trust assets left to the child until such time as the child, or children if there is more than one, reaches the age at which he is entitled to receive the trust assets, as specified in the trust agreement. This will greatly add to the task of the successor trustee as he will need to ensure that the trust assets are properly invested and secured for the period of the child's trust as well as make provision from time to time for the welfare, upkeep and education of the child. Only when the last child reaches the age specified in the trust document can the successor trustee formally distribute the remaining assets and wind down the living trust. This may well be years or even decades after the grantor has passed away......

Conclusion

The length of time that it takes to settle the trust and distribute assets is often dependent on whether an estate tax return is due. If a return will be due, then it is typically prudent to wait until after a closing letter is received from the IRS to make final distributions. This can take up to 18 months from the date of the grantor's death where the estate is audited. However, if no estate tax is due, the trust may be wrapped up in a number of months; assuming of course that there are no on-going trusts established under the terms of the living trust itself.

 Resource!

For further information on living trusts see our book entitled "How to Make a Living Trust & Avoid Probate", details of which are set out on page 310.

INDEX

T

Other Great Books from Enodare's Estate Planning Series

Make Your Own Last Will & Testament

By making a will, you can provide for the distribution of your assets to your love ones, appoint guardians to care for your children, provide for the management of gifts to young adults and children, specify how your debts are to be paid following your death, make funeral arrangements and much more.

This book will guide you through the entire process of making a will. It contains all the forms that you will need to make a valid legal will, simply and easily.

Make Your Own Living Trust & Avoid Probate

Living trusts are used to distribute a person's assets after they die in a manner that avoids the costs, delays and publicity of probate. They also cater for the management of property during periods of incapacity.

This book will guide you step-by-step through the process of creating your very own living trust, transferring assets to your living trust and subsequently managing those assets.

All relevant forms are included.

Make Your Own Living Will

Do you want a say in what life sustaining medical treatments you receive during periods in which you are incapacitated and either in a permanent state of unconsciousness or suffering from a terminal illness? Well if so, you must have a living will!

This book will introduce you to living wills, the types of medical procedures that they cover, the matters that you need to consider when making them and, of course, provide you with all the relevant forms you need to make your own living will!

Other Great Books from Enodare's Estate Planning Series

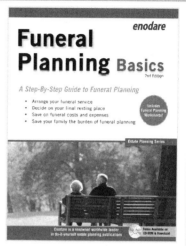

Make Your Own Medical & Financial Power of Attorney

The importance of having powers of attorney is often underappreciated. They allow people you trust to manage your property and financial affairs during periods in which you are incapacitated; as well as make medical decisions on your behalf based on the instructions in your power of attorney document. This ensures that your affairs don't go unmanaged and you don't receive any unwanted medical treatments.

This book provides all the necessary documents and step-by-step instructions to make a power of attorney to cover virtually any situation!

Estate Planning Essentials

This book is a must read for anyone who doesn't already have a comprehensive estate plan.

It will show you the importance of having wills, trusts, powers of attorney and living wills in your estate plan. You will learn about the probate process, why people are so keen to avoid it and lots of simple methods you can actually use to do so. You will learn about reducing estate taxes and how best to provide for young beneficiaries and children.

This book is a great way to get you started on the way to making your own estate plan..

Funeral Planning Basics - A Step-By-Step Guide to Funeral Planning

Through proper funeral planning, you can ensure that your loved ones are not confronted with the unnecessary burden of having to plan a funeral at a time which is already very traumatic for them.

This book will introduce you to issues such as organ donations, purchasing caskets, cremation, burial, purchasing grave plots, organization of funeral services, legal and financial issues, costs of pre-arranging a funeral, how to save money on funerals, how to finance funerals and much more.

www.enodare.com

Will Writer - Estate Planning Software

Everything You Need to Create Your Estate Plan

Product Description

Enodare's Estate Planning Software helps you create wills, living trusts, living wills, powers of attorney and more from the comfort of your own home and without the staggering legal fees!

Through the use of a simple question and answer process, we'll guide you step-by-step through the process of preparing your chosen document. It only takes a few minutes of your time and comprehensive help and information is available at every stage of the process.

Product Features:

 Last Wills

Make gifts to your family, friends and charities, make funeral arrangements, appoint executors, appoint guardians to care for your minor children, make property management arrangements for young beneficiaries, release people from debts, and much more.

 Living Trusts

Make gifts to your family and friends, make property management arrangements for young beneficiaries, transfer assets tax efficiently with AB Trusts, and much more.

 Living Wills

Instruct doctors as to your choices regarding the receipt or non-receipt of medical treatments designed to prolong your life.

Healthcare Power of Attorney

Appoint someone you trust to make medical decisions for
you if you become mentally incapacitated.

 ### Power of Attorney for Finance and Property

Appoint someone you trust to manage your financial affairs if you become mentally
incapacitated, or if you are unable to do so for any reason.

 ### And More.........

Enodare's Will Writer software also includes documents such as self-proving Affidavits,
Deeds of Assignment, Certifications of Trust, Estate Planning Worksheet, Revocation forms
and more.

The documents are valid in all states except Louisiana.

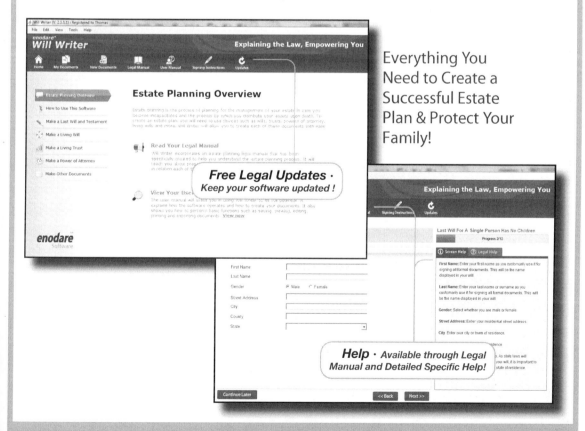

Everything You
Need to Create a
Successful Estate
Plan & Protect Your
Family!

www.enodare.com

Entrepreneur's Guide to Starting a Business

Entrepreneur's Guide to Starting a Business takes the fear of the unknown out of starting your new business and provides a treasure chest of information that will help you be successful from the very start.

First-time entrepreneurs face a daunting challenge in identifying all of the issues that must be addressed and mastered when starting a new business. If any item slips through the cracks, or is handled improperly, it could bring a new company crashing to the ground. Entrepreneur's Guide to Starting a Business helps you meet that challenge by walking you through all of the important aspects of successfully launching your own business.

When you finish reading this book, not alone will you know the step-by-step process needed to turn your business idea and vision into a successful reality, but you'll also have a wealth of practical knowledge about corporate structures, business & marketing plans, e-commerce, hiring staff & external advisors, finding commercial property, sales & marketing, legal & financial matters, tax and much more.

- Comprehensive overview of all major aspects of starting a new business

- Covers every stage of the process, from writing your business plan to marketing and selling your new product

- Plain English descriptions of complex subject matters

- Real-world case study showing you how things play out in an actual new business environment

NEW TITLE

Personal Budget Kit

Budgeting Made Easy

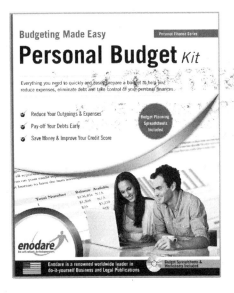

In this kit, we'll guide you step-by-step through the process of creating and living with a personal budget. We'll show you how analyze how you receive and spend your money and to set goals, both short and long-term.

You'll learn how to gain control of your personal cash flow. You'll discover when you need to make adjustments to your budget and how to do it wisely. Most of all, this kit will show you that budgeting isn't simply about adding limitations to your living but rather the foundation for living better by maximizing the resources you have.

This Personal Budget Kit provides you with step-by-step instructions, detailed information and all the budget worksheets and spreadsheets necessary to identify and understand your spending habits, reduce your expenses, set goals, prepare personal budgets, monitor your progress and take control over your finances.

- Reduce your spending painlessly and effortlessly

- Pay off your debts early

- Improve your credit rating

- Save & invest money

- Set & achieve financial goals

- Eliminate financial worries

Budget Planning Spreadsheets Included

enodare

NEW TITLE